1,001
Ways to Live
WILD

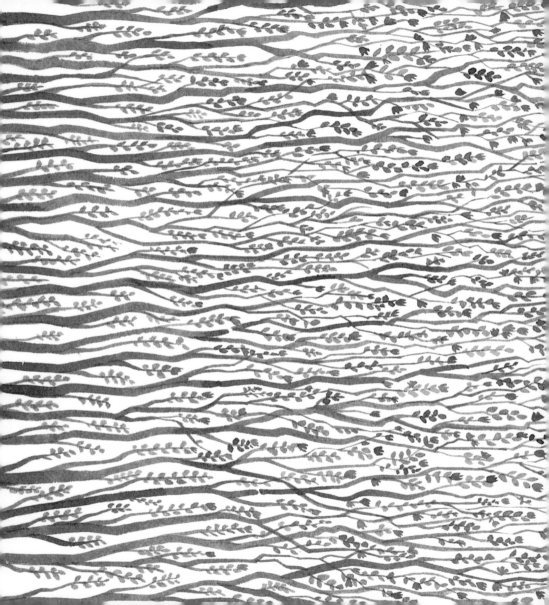

1,001 Ways to Live WILD

A LITTLE BOOK OF EVERYDAY ADVENTURES

Barbara Ann Kipfer

Illustrations by
Francesca Springolo

■ **NATIONAL GEOGRAPHIC**

Washington, D.C.

Published by National Geographic Partners, LLC.

ISBN: 978-1-4262-1666-4

Since 1888, the National Geographic Society has funded more than 12,000 research, exploration, and preservation projects
around the world. National Geographic Partners distributes a portion of the funds it receives from your purchase
to National Geographic Society to support programs including the conservation of animals and their habitats.

Become a member of National Geographic and activate
your benefits today at natgeo.com/jointoday.

National Geographic Partners, LLC.
1145 17th Street NW
Washington, DC 20036-4688 USA

For information about special discounts for bulk purchases, please contact
National Geographic Books Special Sales: ngspecsales@ngs.org

For rights or permissions inquiries, please contact National Geographic Books
Subsidiary Rights: ngbookrights@ngs.org

Interior design: Sanáa Akkach/Katie Olsen

Printed in China

15/RRDS/1

*I dedicate this book
to my wild and crazy
support team: Paul Magoulas,
Kyle Kipfer, and Keir Magoulas.
Thank you also to my friend
and colleague Bob Amsler,
whose wild programming skills
are unmatched.*

Introduction

What does it mean to live wild? We might think of a lion lumbering gracefully across the Serengeti, its mane blowing in the wind. Or we might envision a skydiver experiencing the thrill and exhilaration of flying when leaping from an airplane. What if we could experience such grace and beauty and excitement and freedom in our everyday lives?

This book offers 1,001 little ways to do just that—to turn each day into an adventure. You will discover a fun and heartfelt list of musings, things to do, inspirational quotes, and *wild* tidbits of knowledge. Each idea suggests a way to bring more passion, play, and courage into your life.

For me, writing this book came at a great time. My husband and I are adjusting to an empty nest while contemplating what to do with our later years. Our sons are adjusting to being out-of-nesters with no one to tell them what to do! This got me thinking about the many turning points in life: graduations, first jobs, big birthdays, relationship beginnings and endings, marriage, parenthood, retirement—and the list goes on. There are so many stages at which we rethink what we want out of life. I hope this book will help jump-start anyone who is approaching a new beginning or needs a jolt of "get out there and live."

The entries in this book are serendipitously offered, so you can either read straight through or go wild(!) browsing them. Many ideas encourage travel, appreciation of nature, and trying new activities. But as you read, remember that a lot of "living wild" happens in your mind when you pay attention to the extraordinary beauty that surrounds you every day. At its heart, living wild is about experiences, not places. It is about living a freer, more joyful and fulfilling life.

1. Dance in a public fountain.

🖋

2. Write the opening sentence
of your debut novel.

🖋

3. Enter a sand castle–building contest.
Build the most impressive one you can.

🖋

4. Don't get ready. Don't get set.
Just go!

5. At dawn, take an hour to witness the transition from night to day. Stop and contemplate the incredible beauty of the everyday.

e

6. Ride a tandem bike with a friend.

e

7. Be a great actor. If you act, think, or speak it, you become it. Spread your wings and soar.

8. Learn to balance on a slackline between two trees. Staying balanced while moving teaches you to focus and let go of tension. You will carry this balance into your daily life.

9. Backpack through Europe or another continent.

10. Explore the never ending vineyards of California's wine country.

11. Appreciate the beauty of water trickling from a tap.

12. Don't let the world in on your secret passion.

13. If you can *be* here, you can be free and happy right here and now.

14. Mend a broken heart by hitting
the trail for a week.

15. Drive through towns and villages
you have never seen before.

16. Introduce yourself to someone you know
but never speak to: a neighbor, a shopkeeper,
or a colleague, for example.

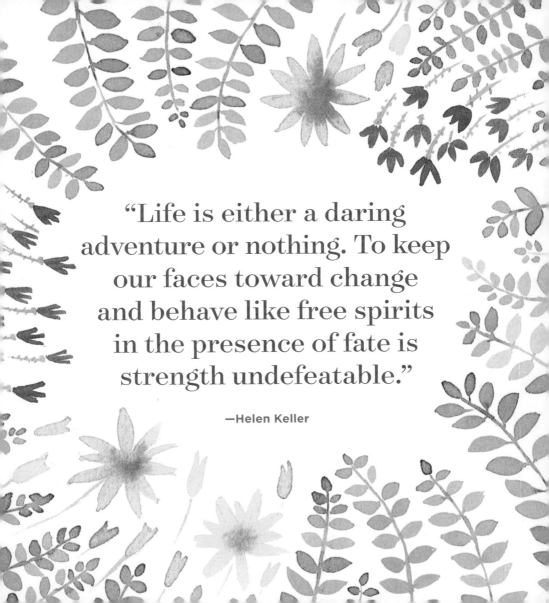

"Life is either a daring adventure or nothing. To keep our faces toward change and behave like free spirits in the presence of fate is strength undefeatable."

—Helen Keller

17. Repair a hole in a window screen. It's a major accomplishment to fix something yourself.

18. Go to a busy place and walk with the crowd or walk aimlessly through it. Instead of walking with a purpose, experience the flow of a place and the people within it.

19. If you don't scale the mountain, you can't view the plain.

20. What part of nature is the most interesting to you? If it is clouds, study them and take photographs. If it is the moon, learn what the names of the full moons are and the lore behind them.

21. Live each day as if it were your last, but learn each day as if you will live forever.

22. Witness a birth of a human or an animal. It's an experience you will never forget.

23. Go kayaking. The rhythmic, steady movement can help release your anxieties and immerse you in a peaceful environment.

ම

24. Have the courage to let yourself be happy.

ම

25. Go to bartending school for a week or learn how to mix perfect cocktails.

26. Learn to find your way by using the stars as your guide—just as ancient sailors crossed the seas and adventurers explored the land.

ɘ

27. Figure out how to gracefully go to the bathroom in the woods.

ɘ

28. To fully experience life, connect with something larger than your individual self.

Adventure Skills to Cultivate

Navigation
Being able to read a compass and paper map ensures you'll not get lost.

First Aid
Knowing how to treat wounds and injuries is a primary way in which you act to survive.

Sky Reading
Navigating by the sun, moon, and stars means you can find your way, even off the grid, where your GPS can't help you.

Finding Food
Put protein in your diet by learning to catch fish or small game.

Foraging

Identify edible plants so you can find food without
having to kill anything.

Weather Forecasting

Fascinating wind and cloud patterns can help you know
when you are safe and when you need to take shelter.

Shelter Building

Creating a lean-to from nature's castoffs offers
you shade, warmth, and protection.

Knot Tying

Knowing how to tie basic knots can secure food, supplies, and shelter.

Water Purification

Find out how to locate clean water and use a water purifier
in case you run out of the elixir of life.

Fire Building

A campfire gives you warmth, light, cooked food, and … s'mores.
Properly dousing a fire protects our wildlands.

29. Read a short adventure novel
in a long day.

30. Remember that you are responsible
for your own experience. Nobody can tell you
if what you are doing is good, meaningful,
or worthwhile.

31. Eat slowly and savor the moment.

32. Camp in the desert, on high ground.

33. Peruse a photo album of
your past adventures.

⊚

34. Ride a boogie board.

⊚

35. Learn how to read the runway signals
at the airport.

⊚

36. When someone annoys you, say absolutely
nothing for one minute. To pause instead
of react feels very empowering.

37. An adventure can be simple. Hike, ice-skate, or go to a football game.

↖

38. Experience an adrenaline rush and a sense of peace during a parachuted free fall from an aircraft.

↖

39. If there's a full moon and you are busy thinking about something else, you do not see the moon. Pay attention to the moon, and your thinking stops naturally.

40. Count your blessings. Seriously.

41. Relax in a Finnish sauna, where steam is generated by pouring water on hot stones.

42. Find a pond or stream and lose yourself watching dragonflies, fish, and frogs.

43. Get certified in first aid, then take it a step further and get certified in wilderness first aid.

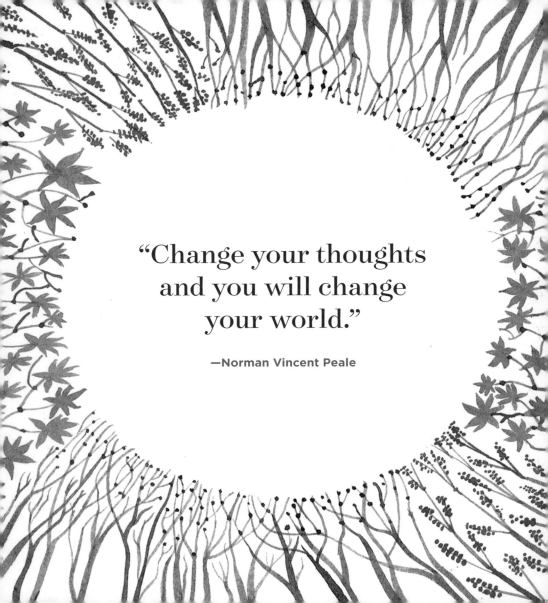

"Change your thoughts
and you will change
your world."

—Norman Vincent Peale

44. Attempt to see things from as many angles as possible.

45. Stargaze.

46. For a day, give a flower to every person you know.

47. If you want the rainbow, put up with the rain.

48. Play in the dirt.
Getting dirty gives you
permission to let go.

ও

49. Garden in January! No matter where
you live, there's a way—even indoors.

ও

50. Go for a run on city streets at night,
when they are gloriously empty
of daytime traffic.

51. Decorate a pair of cheap canvas sneakers with permanent markers. Spray them with a waterproofing solution to protect them in the rain.

❧

52. Walk along the South Rim of the Grand Canyon.

❧

53. Choose meaningful projects that will have a big impact on the way you live. Create things you will use or that beautify your surroundings.

54. Look at a map upside down.
You might see places in a new light.

55. Close your eyes and randomly point
to an entrée on a menu at a restaurant.
Then order it.

56. Embrace change for the sake of it.

57. Challenge the creature of routine
within you.

"The self is not
something one finds;
it is something
one creates."

—Thomas Szasz

58. On the longest day of the year, watch the sun come up at your favorite outdoor spot.

e

59. Learn how to humanely lasso a calf or how to do the Texas Skip, an impressive rope trick.

e

60. There's no better way to put life back in perspective than to spend a few days living in the great outdoors. Bone up on survival skills and leave your fancy camping gear behind.

61. Sleep on a beach.

62. It can be thrilling (really!) to clean out your entire abode and hold a yard sale. Give away whatever you don't sell.

63. Invent a new sandwich made from your favorite foods.

64. Flip (or scroll) to a random page in the local college's course catalog. Sit in on a class on that page.

65. Write a thank-you note to your
most influential teacher.

66. Listen to a shortwave radio.
In solitude and silence, you will hear
hundreds of voices murmuring,
in unknown or unrecognizable languages,
speaking unendingly. You can imagine
them and their worlds.

67. Bike through a city.
You will understand its geography
in a way that a motorist never will.

68. The more attention you bring to
the direct experience of eating,
the more interesting it becomes.

69. Don't listen to criticism
from others or from yourself.

70. Sit in a tree in silence.

71. Walk in one direction for an entire day,
from sunrise to sunset. Pick up a rock at
the beginning and leave the rock
at the end of the walk.

Wild "Life Lists" to Make

Animals, including the endangered, vulnerable,
and threatened

Birds' eggs and nest identification

Butterfly and moth sightings, by location, date, and species

Insects: the most unusual (not for the squeamish)

The mycological world: mushrooms, fungi, and lichen

Plants: native, edible, and the ones you'd like to see

Rocks and minerals: one of the best because
you can take specimens home

Seashells: a collection you can display

Stars and planets: identify and locate celestial objects using maps

Trees: note leaf shapes, bark, seeds, and nuts

72. Happiness comes when you are aware of the natural wonders around you.

ℯ

73. Learn how to make a sun compass or improvise a magnetic compass. Navigate using your watch.

ℯ

74. Change is life and it is all around you.

ℯ

75. Don't listen to a bully.

76. Attend a car show.

ϒ

77. Visit a casino with a pocketful of quarters. It is a low-risk way to experience gambling.

ϒ

78. Have a take-out party, where guests bring homemade versions of their favorite Chinese dishes.

ϒ

79. Self-reliance is emboldening. Recognize some of the little things that you can do for yourself.

80. Tour historic buildings
in your hometown.

81. Visit real estate open houses.
We all like to peek behind
closed doors sometimes.

82. Eat honey straight from the jar.

83. Drink milk straight from the carton.

84. Do one thing to get more involved with your community.

85. Go to a parade.

86. Attend a chili cook-off. Eat the spiciest chili you can bear.

87. Plant a tree.

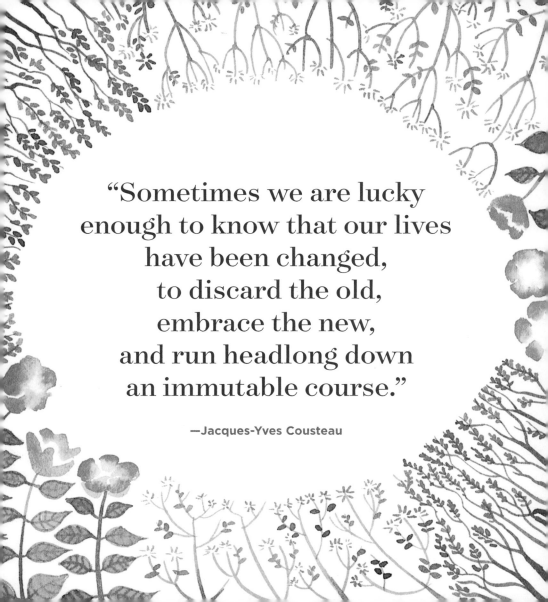

"Sometimes we are lucky
enough to know that our lives
have been changed,
to discard the old,
embrace the new,
and run headlong down
an immutable course."

—Jacques-Yves Cousteau

88. Master a pub game, such as darts, pool, or trivia.

89. Go on an Amazon River cruise.

90. Lose yourself in live music as often as possible. Check out a new club or a free outdoor concert every week.

91. Try to talk like Yoda.

92. Build the ultimate tree house.

93. Concoct dandelion wine.
You only need basic ingredients such as
water, yeast, sugar, and lemons or oranges.

94. Run wildly down the sand dunes
and into the frothing surf.

95. Be the eyewitness of all you see.

96. Pick a route that takes twice the time
to reach the exact same place.

97. Travel to destinations off the grid
and hidden from view.

98. The courage and discipline
you need to consider every action,
thought, and word carries over
to everything you do.

99. Make your ears into
"listening antennas," especially in
crowds or social situations.
You will learn more by speaking less.

100. Select a magazine you've never heard
of from a newsstand.

101. Hike pristine wilderness with friendly
porters and guides.

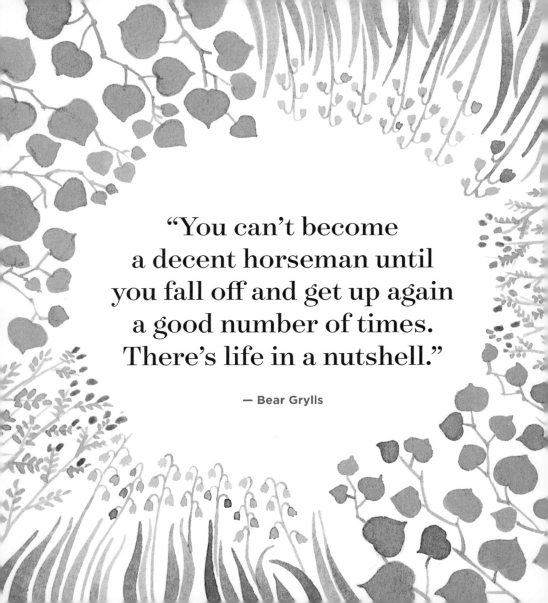

"You can't become
a decent horseman until
you fall off and get up again
a good number of times.
There's life in a nutshell."

— Bear Grylls

102. Land a skateboard trick.

103. Learn to snowboard.

104. Make mistakes on purpose,
to remind yourself that there is
no perfection.

105. Leave funny notes in library books.

106. Cross the Cumberland Gap of the Appalachian Mountains, following Daniel Boone's Wilderness Road to the West.

e

107. Learn how to fold a fitted sheet.

e

108. In *Ulysses,* James Joyce retained typos and misspellings and skipped punctuation to make his prose more insightful.

109. Practice blind contour drawing. Move your eye along an object's edge and move your pencil the same way on paper. Don't look down until you are done! Then repeat. This is a challenging but surprisingly satisfying activity.

e

110. Volunteer for a wildlife conservation organization.

e

111. Invite friends over for an impromptu come-as-you-are and bring-whatever-is-in-your-kitchen party.

Spicy Foods to Try

Bibimbap with kimchi, a Korean stirred-rice dish

Caribbean jerk chicken with rice, plantains,
carrots, and green beans

Cau-cau, a Creole tripe stew served with rice

Huo guo, translated as "hot pot" and common
in Asian countries

Kimchi *jjigae,* a stewlike Korean dish, full of kimchi,
tofu, veggies, and pork

Pad prik khing, a Thai red curry stir-fry

Papa a la Huancaína, Peruvian boiled yellow
potatoes in a spicy cream sauce

Phaal curry, a British Asian Indian curry dish

Sambal oelek, a chili paste made with mortar
and pestle in Indonesian kitchens

Shrimp Creole, a Louisiana dish of shrimp
in a spicy tomato sauce, served on rice

Spicy tuna rolls, sushi made with chili spice

Tom yum, a Lao and Thai clear, spicy,
and sour soup

Vindaloo, a staple of curry-house menus

Wot, an Ethiopian spicy stew
with meat and lentils

Suicide chicken wings, deep-fried and
drenched in an intense sauce

112. Nurture a garden, a pet, or a child. The rewards are numerous.

113. Create your own Ministry of Silly Walks, as in the *Monty Python's Flying Circus* television show.

114. Picnic on a beach.

115. If you look at life as an adventure, then it will be.

116. Select your day's activities based on one letter of the alphabet.

117. Whistle on a blade of grass.

118. Have fun without spending any money today. How wild would that be?

119. Squeeze a mini-adventure into a business trip.

120. Climb a (quiet) volcano.

121. Elope.

122. Skip down the middle of a street.

123. Make a practice of putting money into an adventure fund every month.

124. Enjoy your eccentricities and those
of other people.

ॐ

125. In Japan, nutmeg or cinnamon
are added to office HVAC systems to enhance
productivity. Place potpourri on your desk
at work to amp up your energy and alertness.

ॐ

126. Design your own logo. Have it printed
on a coffee cup and T-shirt.

"Mix a little foolishness
with your prudence;
it's good to be silly
at the right moment."

—Horace

127. Check out the view from the highest spot in your county or state.

128. Hang a photo exhibition in an unusual place—a bathroom stall or old phone booth.

129. Cook a big Thanksgiving, Christmas, Easter, Passover, or Fourth of July meal during a completely different season.

130. Learn to read tea leaves.

ᒋ

131. Calculate how far it is to a dream destination from your house. Make a sign that says, "Sedona, Arizona: 2,175 Miles."

ᒋ

132. Go on a night hike to see a place you know from a completely different perspective.

ᒋ

133. Read something inspiring before bedtime to create exciting dreams.

134. Walk with a toddler. A toddler does not understand the concept of walking as a function. It is a chance to amble about, staring and marveling at things. Embrace the way a toddler follows one impulse of curiosity after another.

ꙅ

135. To make the right decisions, you must be free to make the wrong ones.

ꙅ

136. Kiss someone in the rain . . . a slow-motion kiss.

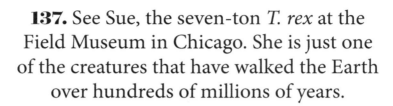

137. See Sue, the seven-ton *T. rex* at the Field Museum in Chicago. She is just one of the creatures that have walked the Earth over hundreds of millions of years.

-¦-

138. Follow your heart's desire and it will lead you to great adventures.

-¦-

139. Notice everything. Everything is interesting.

-¦-

140. Throw yourself into a slightly daunting creative project.

Wild List

Fun Festivals to Attend

Austin City Limits (Fall; Austin, Texas)

Blue Ridge BBQ & Music Festival (June; Tryon, North Carolina)

Cheyenne Frontier Days (July; Cheyenne, Wyoming)

Fourth of July (Seward, Alaska, or Bristol, Rhode Island)

GoPro Mountain Games (June; Vail, Colorado)

Maine Lobster Festival (July; Rockland, Maine)

Moab Arts Festival (May; Moab, Utah)

Muddy Buddy Adventure Series (nine U.S. cities)

Reggae on the River (summer; Humboldt County, California)

Sasquatch! Music Festival (May; Quincy, Washington)

141. Run with the bulls in
Pamplona, Spain.

142. Ride a mechanical bull in a tavern.

143. Take a creative workshop.

144. Use your sense of touch to choose
an outfit by texture rather than by sight.

145. Learn how to right a capsized
kayak—and get back in.

146. Look at something through
a magnifying glass. You'll find beauty
where you least expected.

147. Meditate. You will live more
authentically in the present moment.

148. Take a week of coaching sessions
in a new sport.

149. Learn to play a musical instrument.

150. Skip stones across water.

151. Visit every state park in your state.
Take photographs and journal
your experience.

152. Experience the winter solstice at Newgrange, a Stone Age monument in Ireland.

↖

153. Go to a local sporting event.

↖

154. Get an autograph from your favorite athlete.

↖

155. Care less about what other people think.

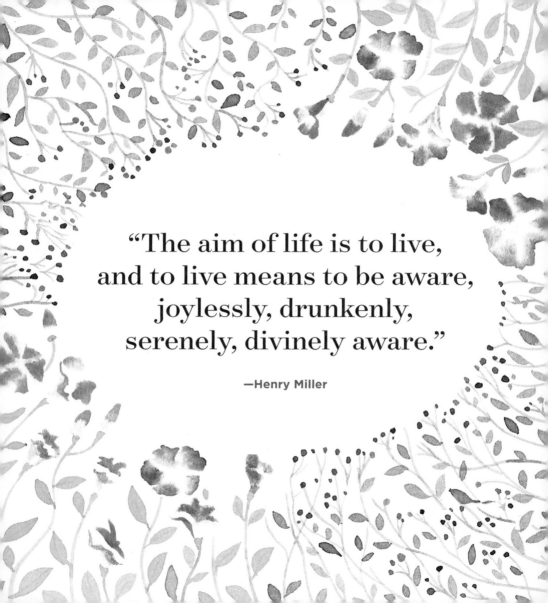

"The aim of life is to live, and to live means to be aware, joylessly, drunkenly, serenely, divinely aware."

—Henry Miller

156. Dare not to think. Observe your thoughts as if they are passing clouds.

157. Charisma is passion demonstrated.

158. Live your life like a competent captain: Set a course and steer your boat when necessary, but let the wind and waves do most of the work.

159. Tour an airplane factory.

160. Have a dance night at least once a month
by yourself or with friends.

ॐ

161. Don't wait for your ship to come in;
row out and get it.

ॐ

162. Experience life as an adventure.
Resist the temptation to explain everything.

ॐ

163. Notice the sound track of the day shift
from birdcalls to a nocturnal chorus.

164. Take a photo of the same scene each day. It is an exercise in noticing the little changes in everyday things.

✌

165. Go camping alone.
Bring exactly what you need.

✌

166. Line a sidewalk with luminarias.

✌

167. Spend at least one day each week by yourself, doing what you want to do. Learn the difference between being alone and being independent.

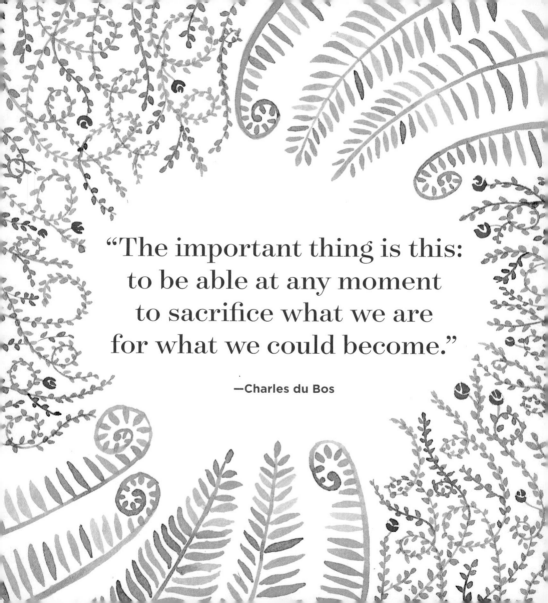

"The important thing is this: to be able at any moment to sacrifice what we are for what we could become."

—Charles du Bos

168. Reclaim your Sundays as a day
for rest or fun rather than
for housework or errands.

G

169. Do circuit training instead of slogging
through 30 minutes on a treadmill.

G

170. Go geocaching—it's a modern-day
treasure hunt. Search online to get the exact
location of more than a million caches
around the world.

171. Forget what your mother told you
and jump on a mattress.

e

172. Eat real butter and real sugar.
Drink whole milk and real cream.
Eat everything in moderation
and ignore the "scary food fact
of the week."

e

173. Disguise one part of yourself for a day:
your voice, your style, your walk, your hair,
or your handwriting. See what happens.

174. Don't be afraid of the mean girl.

175. Allow others to follow your path in the wild. Learn to make international trailblazing symbols from grass, sticks, and rocks.

176. Fast for a day, drinking only sugar water. Observe your mood changes and how you no longer see the world in the same way.

Plants You Can Eat in the Forest

Amaranth
Seeds can be used as cereal or ground into flour for bread.

Burdock
This root vegetable has a sweet, earthy flavor and a tender-crisp texture.

Cattail
With multiple uses at different times of the year,
cattail is like a wild supermarket.

Chickweed
Eaten in salads or cooked, chickweed is also a modest
source of vitamin C.

Chicory
The leaves are eaten as a salad or braised as a vegetable, and the bitter root—
dried and partly caramelized—is often added to coffee.

Clover
These tasty blossoms can be consumed as a survival food.

Curled Dock
The young leaves of this wild vegetable should be boiled
in several changes of water to remove the oxalic acid.

Dandelion
The root can be cooked as a vegetable or may be roasted and used
like coffee. The leaves can be cooked or eaten as salad.

Fiddleheads
These furled fronds of a young fern can be harvested as a vegetable.

Fireweed
Before the plant blooms, young stems can be eaten raw or in salads.

Nettles
The young leaves can be cooked as a vegetable.

Purslane
The moisture-rich leaves are cucumber-crisp and have
a lemony tang with a peppery kick.

177. Have an emergency joke kit at the ready.

178. Go on a local walking tour with an archaeologist. Learn about the people who came before you.

179. Take a hot-air-balloon ride.

180. Learn basic parkour moves. Try a roll and monkey vault.

181. Break a long-distance walk into a series of short strolls.

182. Put your television in a box in the basement.

183. Learn how to tie a cherry stem with your tongue.

184. Bake your own bread, make soup from scratch, catch a fish for your dinner, roll sushi, or build a gingerbread house.

185. Leave happy messages for people under their car windshield wipers.

186. Save the life of an ant.

187. Go to the top of one of the world's tallest buildings.

188. Use only your nondominant hand for a day. This requires you to use the opposite side of your brain.

189. Pull an all-nighter and have fun with it.

ϟ

190. Learn how to track stand on a bicycle to improve your balance.

ϟ

191. Set your alarm clock one minute earlier than your normal wake-up time.

ϟ

192. Go for a walk every morning before work.

193. Team up with friends to paint a group mural on a length of butcher paper.

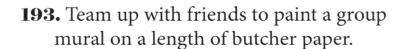

194. Grow plants from clippings, such as lavender, roses, and rosemary.

195. Get trained in CPR. It could make the difference between life and death in an emergency.

196. Set a physical challenge for yourself. You will discover inner strength and overcome your perceived limitations.

"There is no
bad weather,
only inappropriate
clothing."

—Scandinavian proverb

197. Hike a ski slope in the off-season.

198. Watch a sunset from a gondola.

199. Life's adventure is a combination of wonderful, wild ideas and a lot of hard work.

200. Attend a special event at a zoo or aquarium.

201. For a few days every year, step outside your everyday routines and go a bit wild. These are times you will remember.

202. Play an alfresco game of chess in Harvard Square.

203. Your wishbone will never replace your backbone.

204. Send thank-you cards for everything. Be a little old-fashioned about this.

205. Master simple juggling.

206. Revisit a project you abandoned during the past year. How can you make it succeed this time?

207. Go barefoot.

208. Put your camera away and enjoy a sunset. There are enough pictures of sunsets.

209. Every path has its puddle.

210. Experience the wonder of an amazing monastery.

Adrenaline-Pumping Films to See

Apocalypse Now (1979)

The Bourne Identity series

Die Hard series

The French Connection (1971)

Indiana Jones series

Jaws (1975)

Lawrence of Arabia (1962)

Seven Samurai (1954)

The Treasure of the Sierra Madre (1948)

211. Have a good cry.

212. Break out the good china, flowers, tablecloth, and candles for a great meal!

213. Wake up at 3 a.m. to take advantage of the quiet, early morning hours.

214. Everything is difficult at first.

215. Dig a snow cave.

e

216. Learn to set up a snow camp.

e

217. Live life as a today rather than
a yesterday or a tomorrow.

e

218. See an endangered species at a zoo.
Who knows how long it may be around?

219. Read up on something you have always wanted to know more about.

e

220. Take a mini-vacation from a tough workday by noting favorite entries posted on an inspirational website.

e

221. Not knowing is the opposite of ignorance. It means you are aware of what you still have to learn and makes your curiosity grow.

222. Plant rogue wildflowers and bulbs
in unexpected places.

223. Take an off-road jeep tour. Or rent
a jeep and take the wheel.

224. Your strength will grow stronger
by being tested.

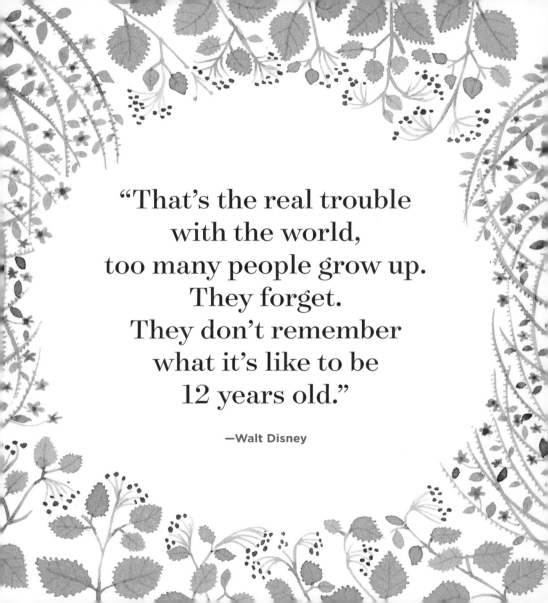

"That's the real trouble
with the world,
too many people grow up.
They forget.
They don't remember
what it's like to be
12 years old."

—Walt Disney

225. Allow yourself to have something
you've wanted for a long time.
If you use it for years and years,
it's money well spent.

226. Set up an orienteering course
in a forest. Race your friends from
one checkpoint to another, using only
a compass and map as your guide.

227. Expand your vocabulary by
one word per day.

228. Know how to swim well.
It could save your life.

229. Draw graffiti.

230. Make a list of five to ten personal strengths and ask yourself which of these feel authentic to you. Now examine each for the level of excitement, yearning, even joy that you feel about it. These feelings indicate your top strengths.

231. Compete in a poetry slam.

232. Compliment people all day and see if it does indeed make a difference.

233. Think how much you could learn by reading a dictionary or an encyclopedia.

234. Take a ride in a vintage biplane.

235. If you always dreamed of performing, dare yourself to give it a go at an open mike night.

Wild List

Ways to Be Brave

Risk being wrong.

Tell someone you love how you feel.

Audition for something.

Trust your instincts.

Say "I don't know."

Leave a bad situation.

Start over.

Reinvent yourself.

End a fight.

Spend zero minutes thinking about
the past or future.

236. An afternoon spent chatting with a shop owner in a new city may be more memorable than visiting a tourist attraction.

237. Become more curious. Ask: What does it mean? Why does it matter? Whom does it impact?

238. Collect sand from each beach you visit.

239. Alter your course often.

ꜟ

240. Don't waste time dwelling on
what might have happened if you'd taken
a different path. You'll never know.
You do have the chance to find out what
will happen if you keep moving forward,
choosing each new direction
with care and a positive attitude.

ꜟ

241. Go bird-watching.

ꜟ

242. Learn to identify flowers and trees.

243. Go sledding.

ॐ

244. Try not to say anything
negative today.

ॐ

245. Take a solo road trip.

ॐ

246. Travel to another country
by yourself.

247. Take a whole summer off,
as you did when you were a kid.

248. Go on an eco-friendly vacation.

249. Get pampered with
a hot-stone massage.

250. Get swept up by the passion
of the fans at a major sporting event.

"There *are* no little things.
'Little things,' so called,
are the hinges
of the universe."

—Fanny Fern, *Ginger-Snaps*

251. Get rid of anything negative in your home, from clothes that no longer fit to old love letters from people you'd rather forget. Letting go of the past opens up your future.

252. Speak to someone you've known forever about something you've never discussed.

253. Go fishing.

254. Take a rock-climbing class.

255. Pay attention to the room tone,
or wild track, the barely audible noises
that make up a background sense of quiet.

256. If you bring mindfulness to all parts
of your day, the imagined divide between life
and work disappears and there is no need
to seek a balance. It already exists—
and every part of your day is yours to enjoy.

257. Learn how to clean a lobster,
peel and devein a shrimp, crack
a Dungeness crab, and shuck an oyster.

258. Get over things.

259. Master the free throw on
the basketball court.

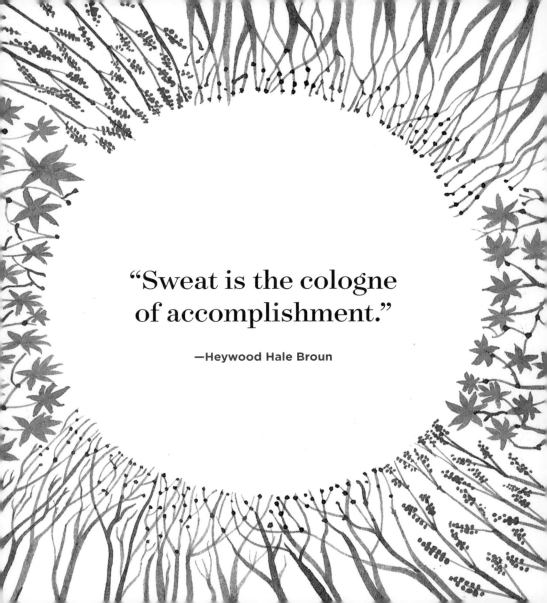

"Sweat is the cologne
of accomplishment."

—Heywood Hale Broun

260. Imagine a book you would like to write. If you think you have a book in you, you do.

↖

261. Do twice the number of sit-ups as you think you can.

↖

262. Read a book in the location where the story takes place.

263. Volunteer for something you don't know how to do. Organizations will happily train you, so you will learn a new skill and help others.

264. Line up funny items in a public place— and know that someone will get a kick out of the display.

265. Treat yourself like a precious flower. Put on sunscreen and spend as much time as possible in the sun today.

266. Try the new restaurant that everyone has been raving about.

ༀ

267. Release a sky lantern.

ༀ

268. Savor a sunset in the wilderness.

ༀ

269. Let go of thinking that you are just not ready. Do it!

270. Indulge in wild imaginings, transformative dreams, and perfect calm.

ↄ

271. Ride an elephant.

ↄ

272. Have a no-TV and no-movie weekend. Do some pre-TV- and pre-movie-era activities.

ↄ

273. Try anything once.

Wild List

Life-Changing Places to Experience

Africa
Taking a genuine African safari is quite a bit more adventurous than driving through a safari park.

Archaeological Site
Unearthing artifacts at an archaeological dig can be the beginning of a lifelong avocation.

Great Wall of China
Go soon to experience the feats of construction, engineering, and strategy at this now endangered place.

Greece
This country and its islands offer inspiring landscapes, architecture, and waters—as well as the uncanny feeling of being in another time.

Hawaii

Venture to this fleet of islands anchored in the middle of a great ocean.

National Parks

A few days at a major national park like Yellowstone will make you yearn to visit every other national park.

New Zealand

The rolling hills, circuits, and tracks are a dream location for trekkers and campers.

North or South Pole

See the magnificence of frigid deserts and the depth of the ice in the Arctic or Antarctic.

The Ocean

Subject to all the forces of nature, sailing is the ultimate in slow travel.

Paris

Visit a center of creativity and romance in food, architecture, and art.

274. Throw a dart at a map and travel
to wherever it lands.

e

275. Hike through New England
forests as the leaves turn into
a kaleidoscope of colors.

e

276. Leave your inhibitions
at the airport and get into a destination.
Spend days with the locals
and learn what their lives are about.

277. Trek to the Mount Everest base camp and take in views of the world's highest mountain. If you can't get there, climb the highest mountain in your state.

e

278. Put new photographs in all your picture frames.

e

279. Go for a ride in a huge limousine.

280. Forget what you think you know and let the world take you by surprise.

281. You can feel a lot of joy in just walking. Invest all of your body and mind into your steps, and you will be fully in the moment.

282. Look at the world as if it is a puzzle. Try to figure out the meaning of this puzzle.

"To see a World
in a Grain of Sand /
And a Heaven
in a Wild Flower."

—William Blake,
"Auguries of Innocence"

283. Do a handstand against a tree.

284. Learn how to assemble a debris hut and lash together a swamp bed.

285. If you live in a dry area, firescape your yard.

286. Skim across the water on a kitesurfing board.

287. Learn to escape from a straitjacket, handcuffs, or another magician's contraption.

288. Create a Zen rock garden.

289. Teach a kid how to ride a bike.

290. Teach a 16-year-old how to drive a car.

ɣ

291. Paddle a canoe.

ɣ

292. Ride a bus the full length of the route.
You will surely see things you have
never seen before.

ɣ

293. Live with a sense of urgency
and complete awareness.

294. Enjoy the blank pages of a new diary. It's filled with fresh starts and unimagined adventures.

❨

295. Live in another country for a year.

❨

296. Remember: You have to fail. It is the only way to succeed.

❨

297. Let a dog walk you.

Wild List

Trailblazers to Learn About

Hiram Bingham

Christopher Columbus

James Cook

Charles Darwin

Amelia Earhart

Leif Erikson

John Goddard

Mary Leakey

Meriwether Lewis and William Clark

David Livingstone and Henry Stanley

Ferdinand Magellan

298. Play a game of cards in a New York speakeasy.

299. Scramble through the wilderness with or without a GPS.

300. Overnight in a funky historic hotel.

301. If you could do anything in this world right now, what would it be? Ignore cost, skill, or anything that might hold you back.

302. Live as if you are on vacation, savoring every minute and collecting memories like snapshots.

303. Get a spontaneous haircut or curl your hair if it is straight (or vice versa).

304. Don't wait for the next power outage to take a day off from connectedness. Power down, unplug, and hide (if you have to).

305. Forget the cold. Wrap yourself up, go outside, and do something you would usually never do in the winter.

306. For one day, do only one thing at a time. That's wild!

307. Read *The Boy Scout Handbook* to learn how to cook a campfire meal in aluminum foil instead of in a pot.

308. Learn a native dance in the place where the dance originated.

309. Drive the Pan-American Highway from Prudhoe Bay, Alaska, to Ushuaia, Argentina.

310. Raise a butterfly from a caterpillar.

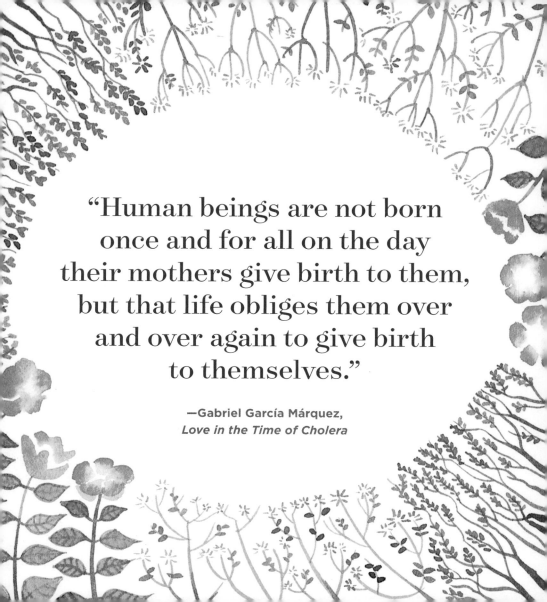

"Human beings are not born once and for all on the day their mothers give birth to them, but that life obliges them over and over again to give birth to themselves."

—Gabriel García Márquez,
Love in the Time of Cholera

311. Create a life-goals list of all the things you want to do or learn. Pick one goal. Then start another list of things you can do to work toward attaining it.

312. Dress up to go see the symphony.

313. Have a bonfire on the beach.

314. Learn to pull a tablecloth out cleanly from a set table.

315. Leave the city of your comfort and go into the wilderness of your intuition.

316. Change the load in a backpack so that it is borne on your hips, not just your shoulders. Your hip and leg muscles are stronger and more able to handle the work.

317. Count to one thousand, which will take a good quarter of an hour and won't be easy. You will appreciate the magnitude of a thousand years.

318. Hang a sign in a public place calling
attention to something in nature.

e

319. Remember that you are not in charge
of anyone or anything other than yourself.
When you finally realize this,
you will be free to live.

e

320. Make a list of your fears.
Then read the list months later, after
the outcomes. Chances are that you will
laugh at what did not come to pass.

321. Foraged food is the ultimate
in local food. Pick berries and vegetables
to make a great meal from Mother Nature.

e

322. Learn to fence.

e

323. Go sand-skimming along a shoreline.

e

324. Remember that most people will forget
what you said but will always remember
how you made them feel.

Adventure Books to Read

Breakfast With Buddha (Roland Merullo, 2008)

Come, Tell Me How You Live (Agatha Christie Mallowan, 2012)

Eat, Pray, Love (Elizabeth Gilbert, 2007)

Journeys of a Lifetime: 500 of the World's Greatest Trips (National Geographic, 2007)

Lonely Planet's 1,000 Ultimate Adventures (Lonely Planet, 2013)

Seven Years in Tibet (Heinrich Harrer, 1952)

The Time Machine (H. G. Wells, 1895)

Vagabonding: An Uncommon Guide to the Art of Long-Term World Travel (Rolf Potts, 2002)

A Walk in the Woods (Bill Bryson, 2006)

Wild (Cheryl Strayed, 2012)

325. Open your house to the evening breeze on hot days and leave it open right up till dawn.

• •

326. Plan a trip to see as much as possible of the Colorado Trail's eight mountain ranges, six national forests, and six wilderness areas.

• •

327. Retrace the route of your favorite sightseeing tour.

• •

328. Try a different topping on your pancakes.

329. Go on a "knowledge adventure," visiting museums that focus on topics you know nothing about.

330. Eat dessert first.

331. Have a picnic in your living room.

332. Think of yourself as a seed or a bulb— totally complete from conception. All that you seek lies within you.

333. Put a message in a bottle
and float it out to sea.

334. Given that there are 168 hours
in a week, if you exercise for an hour
a day, five days a week, that's just
3 percent of your total time.

335. Try a new ethnic food tonight.

336. Binge on live music at a festival.

337. Learn how to write a sentence
in Egyptian hieroglyphs.

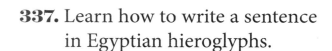

338. Embrace spontaneity.

339. Settle a disagreement with a dance-off,
and you'll see anger replaced with laughter.

340. Build your own boat and sail away
to romance and adventure—
even if it's a toy boat.

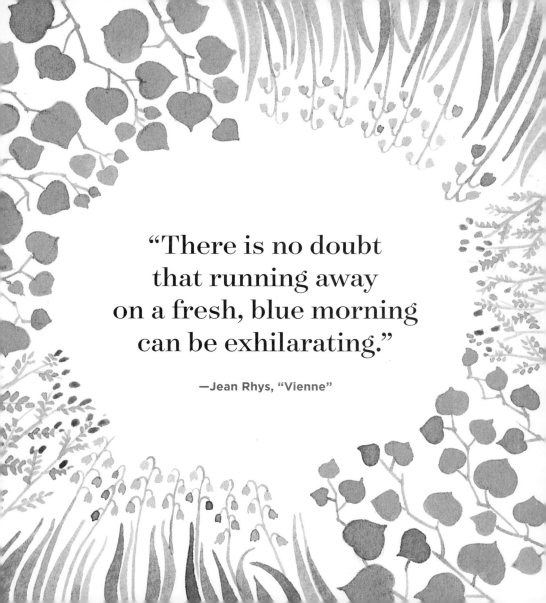

"There is no doubt
that running away
on a fresh, blue morning
can be exhilarating."

—Jean Rhys, "Vienne"

341. Study and practice to pass
a wilderness survival test.

❧

342. Ask yourself: Instead of
buying something, can I either make it
or modify, repair, or reuse what I have?
The answer is often yes, and it can be
a much more interesting solution.

❧

343. Shower with your eyes closed
(but be sure to locate the taps, soap,
and shampoo first).

344. Shadow a chef or construction worker for a day. Learn what it is like to do physical work.

❧

345. Mow your lawn with a push mower. You'll cut down on noise and air pollution while getting a fantastic workout.

❧

346. Have a water fight on a hot summer day.

347. Wear flowers in your hair.

348. Put a great idea in the
suggestion box at work.

349. Read about pioneer women who crossed
the wild North American continent.

350. Choose a wild motto for yourself
and start living by it.

"It's never
too late to have
a happy childhood."

—Tom Robbins,
Still Life With Woodpecker

351. Develop a student mentality.
Commit to lifelong learning, and revel
in the delights of discovery.

ᘒ

352. Buy yourself a bouquet of flowers
at least once a month.

ᘒ

353. Set up a beekeeping station.

ᘒ

354. Find your center and stay there:
It will allow you to live your life
to its maximum.

355. Learn how to surf.

356. Walk in the footsteps of John Muir, from Yosemite Valley to Mount Whitney in California.

357. Eat a different lunch every weekday.

358. Have a nighttime picnic in a garden on a full moon.

359. Enjoy watching the
nocturnal comings and goings
of wildlife.

360. Do something you were
not allowed to do
as a child.

361. Sing at the top of your lungs,
with the windows open.

362. Imagine living your life without the fear of taking risks.

363. Plan a new adventure for each Sunday.

364. Adventure can be as close as a footpath or as expansive as the 2,000-mile Appalachian Trail.

365. Play hide-and-seek, hopscotch, or tag with a child.

Wild List

Animals to See in Person

Elephants
Notice the similarity of an elephant's trunk-shake
to a human handshake and its knees to human knees.

Grizzly Bears
Observe their power and precision as expert anglers.

Kangaroos
These marsupials can hop at speeds up to 35 miles an hour.

Lions
You can hear the male's magnificent roar five miles away.

Manatees
Watch them travel, investigate objects,
and socialize in their watery home.

Meerkats
These catlike carnivores will go to war
to protect their territory.

Pandas
It's great fun to watch them loll
in the sun, play in trees,
and munch on bamboo.

Ring-Tailed Lemurs
You'll have to go to Madagascar (or a zoo)
to see their charismatic behavior.

Tigers
It's amazing to watch these fierce predators
move like oversize house cats.

Whales
Watch them breach, and listen
for their unique song.

366. When you are feeling irritated or annoyed, look around for something yellow. Yellow is a happy color and is also a symbol of clarity, peace, inner strength, and motivation.

367. Call in "sick" on a day you are feeling fabulous.

368. When traveling, explore the sensory differences a new place offers. The stress you may feel in taking in these new experiences is actually your brain moving into high gear.

369. Build an obstacle course
in your backyard and invite the
neighbors over to play.

↖

370. Find time to sweat a few times
per week—it's great for your body
and also your brain.

↖

371. Bake muffins with wild blueberries
you picked yourself.

↖

372. List three things you would like
to accomplish in the next year.
Chart a plan to make them happen.

373. Take an acting workshop.

ও

374. Out in the world, in the street,
in the market, you have a right
to remain closed. Try smiling instead.
When your eyes meet a stranger's,
just smile in a benevolent way.

ও

375. Frame an inspirational print
or photograph and put it where
you will see it often.

ও

376. Climb the 320 steps to the dome top
of St. Peter's Basilica in Vatican City.

377. Cannonball into a pool.

ও

378. Learn to jump-start a car battery
and change a flat tire.

ও

379. Make an exploration list for your life.

ও

380. Train to participate in
a "something-a-thon," such as a marathon,
bike-a-thon, or bowl-a-thon.

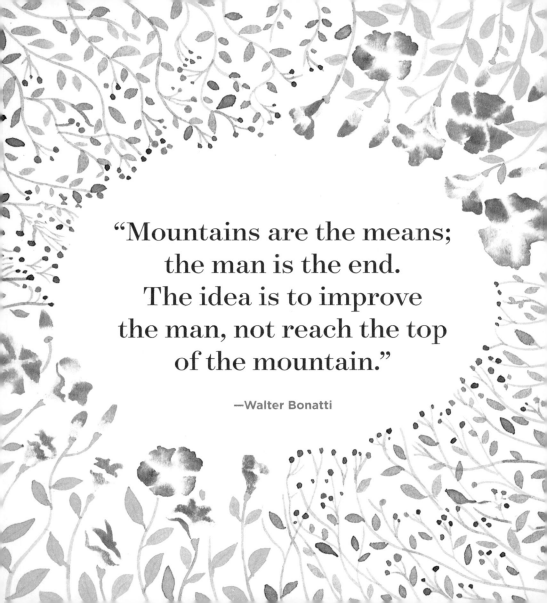

"Mountains are the means;
the man is the end.
The idea is to improve
the man, not reach the top
of the mountain."

—Walter Bonatti

381. Board a bus that is headed beyond the parameters of your guidebook.

382. If you can read, you can live as many lives as you wish.

383. Make your own greeting cards.

384. Weave a maypole.

385. Explore the vast wilderness
of sparsely populated Greenland.

e

386. Peek under the mundane
to find the magical. Be an excavator,
an archaeologist, an explorer.

e

387. Use this statement: I will not compare
myself with others, nor them with me.
I will appreciate myself for what I contribute
and value others' contributions as well.

388. Consider alternating normal walking with short sprints. Try walking for three minutes then doing a burst for one minute. Keep repeating.

☙

389. After a breakup or major disappointment, pick yourself up and move on. Laugh, shrug your shoulders, clean out your home, and get a new outfit and a haircut.

☙

390. Reconcile your differences with someone to bring yourself peace.

391. Create a sculpture out
of found objects.

392. If you want to soar with eagles,
avoid running with turkeys.

393. See your desires as a group
of wild horses pulling you in a cart
that is flying out of control. Take the reins
and tighten them gently but firmly,
slowing the horses and gaining
control of the cart.

Wild Ways to Spend Your Lunch Hour

Take a ballet class or dance class.

Inhale the plant life in an atrium.

Hit the sauna or steam bath.

Visit a local museum or gallery.

Roller- or ice-skate.

Shoot darts or pool.

Learn a foreign language.

Play backgammon or chess in the park.

Take a two-mile walk.

Share lunch with animals at the zoo.

394. Live in a simple, direct way,
without cluttering your mind
with hatred, judgment, worry, doubt,
or want. Choose the experience
of genuine happiness.

395. Read the book *Into the Wild*
and watch the movie.

396. Share your knowledge and skills.
If you can teach something to someone else,
then you truly know what you are doing.

397. You can learn anywhere—
in your car during your daily commute,
on your couch at midnight, or at your desk
first thing in the morning.

398. Cut out addictive substances
for a whole day and see how much
better you feel.

399. You'll never know what you can
do until you try.

400. After being in the hot sun, plunge into cold water. The few seconds of transition create a wild sensation worth exploring.

❨

401. When a raw emotion arises, refuse to go along with it. Regard it as temporary. Try to look at it from the outside, where it will seem laughable and unpleasant.

❨

402. Be comfortable dining at a table for one.

403. Have as much fun as possible.

404. Never doubt your ability
to push yourself.

405. Venture beneath the surface of a lake
or ocean and swim with the fish.

406. Learning a foreign language
is good for your brain.

"Real freedom
lies in wildness,
not in civilization."

—Charles Lindbergh

407. Push your powers of concentration.
Try to peel an apple in your head.
Visualize the fruit, the knife, the cut, the peel,
and the movements with clinical precision
and photographic accuracy.

❦

408. Cruise down lonesome highways
to vivify your senses. Head out by yourself
for an hour or two a week. Notice people,
activities, objects.

❦

409. Seek out an outdoor movie
or concert in the summertime.

410. Learn how to hypnotize someone!

411. When you know what is stopping you, you can start working on a way to get moving.

412. Stay up late to watch a movie, even if you have to get up early.

413. Paint an art car.

414. Become a scavenger of materials that can be recycled for your projects.

415. Welcome each season. With each new beginning, change something in your home or office (or both).

416. Sometimes it brings real satisfaction to be out of reach and left alone. It's a step back into the wild.

417. Go rappelling.

418. Try black-water rafting.

419. Explore glowworm caves
in places like New Zealand.

420. Take a boat tour of a bioluminescent
bay in Puerto Rico.

421. Look at a problem from many angles
instead of tackling it head-on.

Wild List

National Park Landmarks to See

Bering Land Bridge National Preserve (Alaska)

Cape Royal Trail and Angels Window (Grand Canyon, Arizona)

Chimney Rock National Historic Site (Nebraska)

Cumberland Gap National Historical Park
(Kentucky/Tennessee/Virginia)

Denali National Park and Preserve (Alaska)

Devils Tower National Monument (Wyoming)

Grand Teton and the Teton Range's central peaks (Wyoming)

Half Dome (Yosemite, California)

Island in the Sky (Canyonlands, Utah)

422. Blue highways are the smaller,
less traveled roads traditionally shown
in blue ink on road maps.
Pull out a paper map and travel
the blue highways in your world.

423. Take a new route to work.

424. Walk down unfamiliar streets.

425. Be wildly self-reliant.

426. Throw a paper airplane off a very tall building.

427. Go rogue and delete your online presence: Facebook, Twitter, Instagram, and your blog, too!

428. Go an entire weekend without checking the time.

429. Wear a crazy outfit to the grocery store.

430. Rediscover a childlike sense
of fearlessness.

e

431. Anonymously leave flowers
on co-workers' desks.

e

432. Go north to see a moose—
a full-grown male with a handsome
rack of antlers—in the wild.

e

433. Learn how to track the ebb
and flow of tides.

434. Make a video about something that strikes your fancy.

e

435. We spend a lot of time looking for happiness when the world right around us is full of wonder. To be alive and walk on the Earth is a miracle. Beauty calls to us every day and every hour.

e

436. Join an outdoor adventure club.

e

437. Be a part of life, not apart from it.

"Enter the forest
and the boundaries of nations
are forgotten. It may be that
some time an immortal pine
will be the flag of a united
and peaceful world."

—Enos Abijah Mills

438. Keep your travel documents
in the books you read while traveling,
so in the future you will know
where the books have been.

❧

439. Say yes to the good life and no to all
its pale imitations.

❧

440. For a totally different perspective
on a drive, ride in the backseat
of your own car.

❧

441. Tie-dye a T-shirt.

442. Active forgetfulness makes room
for new things.

443. Meditate while focusing
on a candle flame.

444. Line-dry your clothes.

445. Marvel at the little people far below
when you are atop a mountain or looking out
the window of a skyscraper.

446. Practice complete focus in conversation. This means not only listening well but also being willing to openly share your own thoughts, experiences, and emotions when appropriate.

447. Watch nature shows to learn about wildlife.

448. Cut out "must" and "have to" from your vocabulary for one day.

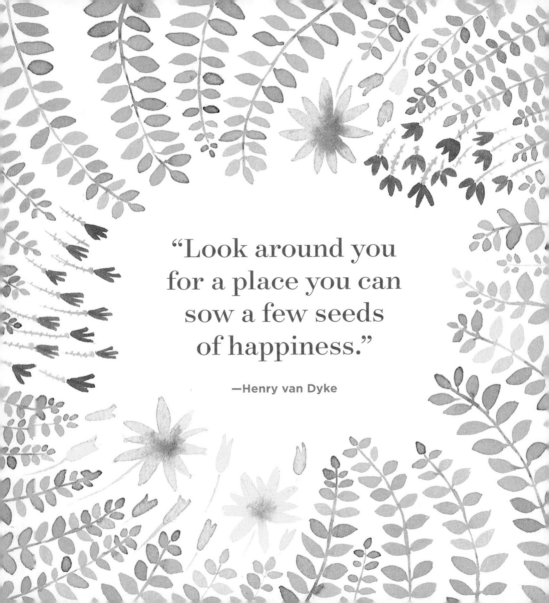

"Look around you
for a place you can
sow a few seeds
of happiness."

—Henry van Dyke

449. Attend flea markets to seek out unique things and unique people.

450. Crash a wedding.

451. Sleep in a castle for a night.

452. Go on a silent retreat.

453. Go an entire day without swearing.
Once you accomplish that,
aim for two days and continue
until you do not swear anymore!

454. Ride on a bullet train.

455. Sunsets are a reminder of the
passing of time. As the sun sets today,
reflect on the day that is
becoming the past.

456. Spend a day or two in the outdoors, watching wildlife, walking in the moonlight, and seeking a truly silent place.

❧

457. Welcome unexpected interruptions, for they may be lead-ins to happy accidents.

❧

458. Thank the heavens for reminding you that life is full of changes and surprises.

Wild Rules to Live By

Do drop any obligation that does not serve you anymore.

Do face your fears.

Do take a road trip with friends or family—
or go alone.

Do think "Why not?" instead of "Why?"

Do spend as much time outside as you possibly can.

Do cook at home more than you eat out.

Do eat "close to the earth" instead of relying
on processed foods.

Do ask "What's the worst thing that can happen?"

Do say yes instead of no.

Don't answer the phone when it rings.

Don't look at the weather forecast each day.

Don't live by a to-do list.

Don't use electronic devices all weekend.

Don't drink and drive.

Don't pollute—with physical objects or bad speech.

Don't waste natural resources.

Don't have expectations.

Don't speak until you have fully listened and paused.

Don't eat unless you are hungry.

459. Learn how to predict the weather
by reading the clouds.

ꙃ

460. Ride a bike across England
in a week.

ꙃ

461. Take a boat into the middle
of a lake and just sit there.

ꙃ

462. Cook in a Hawaiian *imu* pit,
an underground oven.

463. Declare yourself an artist and create a "loft" where you can imagine and design.

ℨ

464. Leap (carefully) off a rock into the water below.

ℨ

465. Buy better and buy less, choosing quality over quantity.

ℨ

466. Learn how to open a pomegranate, dice a mango, pit an avocado, crack a coconut, and cut a pineapple.

467. You are never too old to roast
a marshmallow over a campfire.

468. Look through microscopes
and telescopes to explore
our planet and beyond.

469. Take a camping trip that combines
at least two of the following: backpacking,
orienteering, canoeing, snow hiking,
long-distance bicycling,
or wilderness conservation projects.

470. Compost in your backyard.

471. Have a proper conversation with a kid and learn from the child's innocence.

❀

472. In cold weather, kick up your workout a notch—it will help raise your body temperature.

❀

473. Estimate remaining daylight using your finger widths, the sun, and the horizon.

❀

474. Cultivate a carnivorous plant. Some eat mosquitoes.

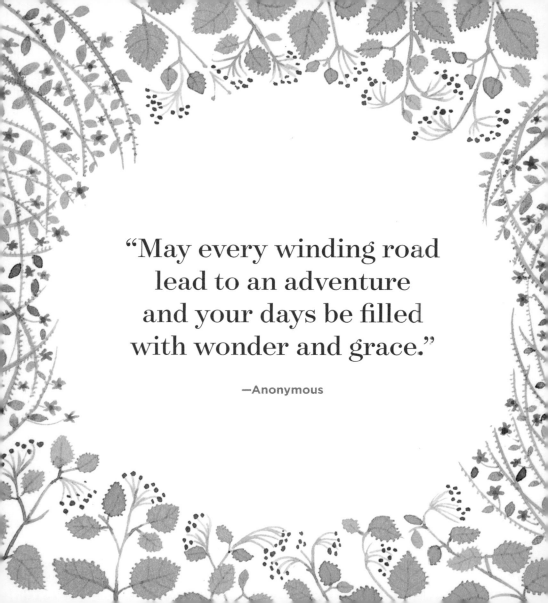

"May every winding road
lead to an adventure
and your days be filled
with wonder and grace."

—Anonymous

475. Before you bring in experts, draw up your own designs for your home renovation. It's your house, it should be your vision.

❧

476. Launch a Kickstarter campaign.

❧

477. Take an "illegal" nap.

❧

478. Next time you get the urge to do something outrageous, give in and do it.

479. Eat alligator meat.
It tastes like chicken.

↖

480. Visit North America's last frontier:
Alaska.

↖

481. Learn how to set up a shade shelter
in a hot place.

↖

482. Know how to pitch a tent
on the beach or in the snow.

483. Underline your favorite passages in books. Donate the books or sell them to a used bookstore so someone else can share your discoveries.

484. Strive to make health-conscious choices. You will feel empowered by treating your body with respect and making deliberate selections.

485. Go on a wine-tasting weekend.

486. Ride a train across America.

487. Cross a desert in a pickup truck.

488. Participate in a sled-dog race.

489. Go snowshoeing.

Natural Phenomena
to Go Wild For

Bioluminescent animals

Salt flats

Currents clashing in maelstroms or vortices

Aurora borealis

Pink lakes

A waterspout at sea

Volcanic lightning

Gigantic crystals in a cavern or mine

Frost flowers

Snow doughnuts

490. Here's a saying to remember:
If you wrestle a bear, never grab for his tail.
In other words, if you get into a difficult
situation, don't make it worse!

491. The next time you attend a party,
leave the host a note saying how much
you enjoyed it and details about why.
Place the note where the host
will definitely find it.

492. Pace yourself, said the turtle to the hare. Hike 50 minutes and rest 10 minutes.

↻

493. Catch a fish bare-handed.

↻

494. Have a séance in a cemetery.

↻

495. Try an iconic cocktail in the city in which it was invented.

496. Book a plane ticket to see that friend who moved away.

e

497. Enjoy walking amid glorious autumn colors.

e

498. Eat something different for breakfast tomorrow.

e

499. Put dry clothing in a plastic bag when you're on a wilderness trip. Chances are, you'll need it.

500. Nothing washes away the
day like a bath.

501. Get a microscopic tattoo.
Only you will know it is there.

502. Photobomb as many photographs as
you can at a popular tourist destination.

503. Avoid talking about your
favorite subject—so it will remain
your favorite subject.

"To Whom It
May Concern—
Only four words of advice:
It can be done."

—Kira Salak

504. Take a selfie in the same spot every year.

505. Don't waste time with a book
you don't love. Pick another.
There are millions out there.

506. Kiss your mate wildly.

507. Take driving lessons at a racetrack
or purchase a ride with a pro driver.

508. Learn how to spin a basketball
on your finger.

509. Find your road less traveled.

510. Pick your own fruits and pumpkins.

511. Go shark-cage diving in Gansbaai,
South Africa.

512. Illustrate your days in a cartoon strip.

513. Sign up for gym classes you have never tried before.

514. Rock out to "Born to Be Wild" by Steppenwolf.

515. You have to give yourself to things to find out if you love them.

516. Figure out what gives you satisfaction and do as much of it as possible.

517. When there is chaos and pandemonium, put in earplugs and enjoy inner peace.

518. Make your own quiet.

519. Seek out a good-news story every day and share it with others.

Physical Challenges to Take

400-meter walk

1-mile walk

1.5-mile run

100 half sit-ups or partial curl-ups

30 push-ups

Sit and reach or V-sit reach

10 pull-ups

Shuttle run

500-yard swim

Bike to a landmark and back

520. Spinning around and around will make you dizzy and giddy.

ⵦ

521. Look for activities that are done not with the expectation of some future benefit but simply because the doing itself is the reward.

ⵦ

522. Suck the marrow from the bones of life.

ⵦ

523. Dowse for water with a Y-shaped stick.

524. Bodysurf a wave.

525. Build a go-kart.

526. Dip into Horatio Alger's inspirational book *Bernard Brooks' Adventures.*

527. To give your brain a workout, use your senses in unexpected ways: Sit outside with your eyes closed or listen to a piece of music while smelling freshly baked cookies.

528. Shop at a farmers market instead of a supermarket.

✳

529. Each morning, ask yourself: How will I be brave today?

✳

530. Participate in laughter yoga.

✳

531. Take a garbage bag on your walk and clean up your environment.

"Only by going too far
can we find out
how far we can go."

—T. S. Eliot

532. Ace a scuba dive ascent.

533. Take the afternoon off and indulge in your guilty pleasures, whatever they may be—cocktails, chocolate, old episodes of *Northern Exposure*.

534. Make a cup out of a folded piece of paper. Investigate what you can do to bring it into reality. If you can imagine something, then it is possible.

535. Being practical gets in the way of fun. Indulge in impracticality!

536. Pick up a new good habit. Practice it for 21 days to make it stick.

537. Watch animals' nocturnal shenanigans during an overnight zoo stay— or in your own backyard.

538. Cook dinner in a solar oven
you make yourself.

❧

539. Answer questions with questions.

❧

540. Find opportunities to incorporate your
passions into your schoolwork or job.

❧

541. Mimic a spa experience at home
by adding aromatic oils and bath salts
to a hot, steaming tub. Follow your bath
with a cold shower.

"A thousand-mile journey begins with a single step."

—Lao Tzu

542. Sneak a fast-food meal
and hide the evidence.

543. Go to a museum and spend an hour
looking at a painting you have
never seen before.

544. Hang a tire swing in your backyard.

545. Dress up for dinner at home,
or even at a pizza parlor.

546. Seek out caves and explore them.

547. If you accept pain, it cannot hurt you.

548. Doing something intensely challenging is an incredible experience. Not doing it when you have the opportunity hurts far more than failing to pull it off.

549. Sing in your own voice.

550. Learn to cook without recipes.

e

551. Simple rules: listen and hear,
speak and mean, eat and taste, care,
give and ask for, have passion
and patience, live and love, laugh.

e

552. No one person can be good
at everything. Find your own talents.

553. Work fewer hours to focus more on personal pursuits.

e

554. Switch up your morning routine.

e

555. Find little ways to replenish yourself every day. Listen to a book on tape during your commute, try some stretches and a cup of tea at 10 a.m. and 2 p.m., or treat yourself to coffee and a croissant for breakfast.

Adventurous Walks to Take

Alphabet Walk

Go for a walk and look for items in alphabetical order.
A is for ant, B is for blue sky, and so on.

Berry Walk

Learn what you can eat and what you can't. Then chow down!

Color Walk

Pick up some paint chips from a home improvement store.
While on your walk, try to find things in nature that match the colors.

Creek Walk

Be sure to wear water shoes and research the creek ahead of time.

Geology Walk

Look around and find where different kinds of rocks appear.
Notice any patterns?

Scavenger Hunt Walk
Make up a list of interesting things to look for, such as
"a house for a mouse" or "a raft for an ant."
Take a child along for even more fun.

Shoreline Walk
Turn over rocks at low tide. You never know
what you might find.

Smell Walk
Take some big breaths and seek out as many
different smells as you can find.

Sound Walk
Request that everyone in your group be as quiet
as possible and listen to all the sounds around them.
After a few minutes, ask each person to share
all the sounds they heard.

Texture Walk
Find five soft things, two prickly things,
three hard things—and add any other textures
you can think of to your list.

556. Knit an outfit for your pet.

557. Say yes to every opportunity today.

558. Make a piece of art and mail it
to your favorite artist.

559. Write a story and send it
to your favorite writer.

560. Release your inner child and play. Twirl a baton, bang a drumstick, or spin a Hula-Hoop around your waist.

561. Learn the six stages of survival: disorientation, urgency, panic, planning, fatigue, and optimism.

562. Learn to identify foods in the wild.

563. Go on a storm-chasing tour in the Great Plains.

564. If you are afraid to roll the dice,
 you will never throw a six.

565. When you lie in a field, you reconnect
 with the Earth without harming it.

566. Learn about wildcrafting—
harvesting plants from their natural habitats
 for food or medicinal purposes.

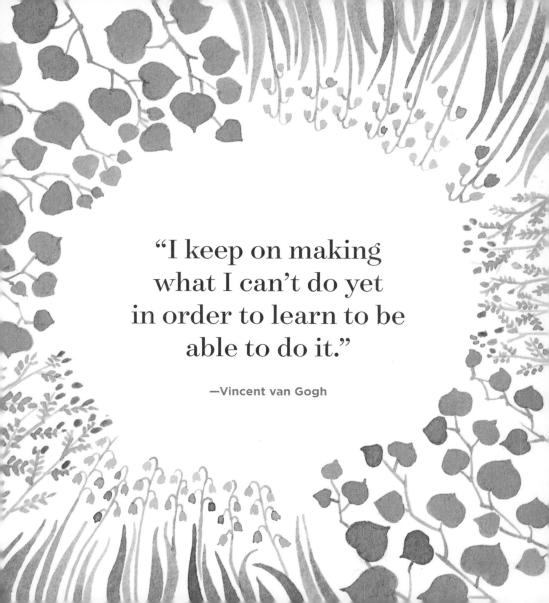

"I keep on making
what I can't do yet
in order to learn to be
able to do it."

—Vincent van Gogh

567. Value the wisdom of trees,
the strength of the wind, the majesty
of mountains, and the serenity
of flowing water.

568. Paint your bedroom a new color.

569. Organize your home according
to the principles of feng shui.

570. Do a handstand underwater.

571. Spend an entire day in your pajamas, just because you can.

572. Touch the Equator.

573. Next time you sit in a traffic jam, start listing things you are happy about.

574. Challenge yourself to hike ten state parks or forests.

575. Discover the pleasure of doing
a kindness for a stranger. Pay for coffee
for the person behind you in line.
Give a book to someone on the bus.

ə

576. Write in a happiness diary every day,
keeping track of good moments in detail,
including your feelings.

ə

577. Sail across an ocean.

578. Plan a grand tour: London, Paris, Rome, Venice, Florence, Lausanne.

ꝺ

579. Cook gourmet food for anyone under 21. Give novice palates something to remember.

ꝺ

580. Organize every room, drawer, and closet in your house.

Adventures to Have on a Rainy Day

Picnic on the living room floor.

Turn the entire house into a maze using blankets, clothespins, and furniture.

Sit alone in a café.

Write long letters to old friends.

Do a jigsaw puzzle.

Walk in the woods.

Listen to old records while you clean out clutter.

Visit the library.

Create an indoor treasure hunt.

581. Parachute or skydive.

♦

582. Walk an unexplored path
and see where it goes.

♦

583. Follow that little dirt road,
zigzagging off in search
of adventure.

♦

584. Make your backyard inviting
for wildlife.

585. Wear noise-canceling headphones and observe a city street. You'll be amazed at the details that you notice.

⊙

586. Learn Morse code so you can send messages to people who speak different languages.

⊙

587. Vacation at a cooking school.

⊙

588. Follow a traditional Chinese recipe to preserve a batch of hundred-year eggs.

589. Watch Hawaiian surfers in winter, when the waves are the biggest.

590. Be a citizen scientist.
You can work with scientists and other volunteers on important research that involves careful observation, measurement, or computation.

591. Take an urban hike.

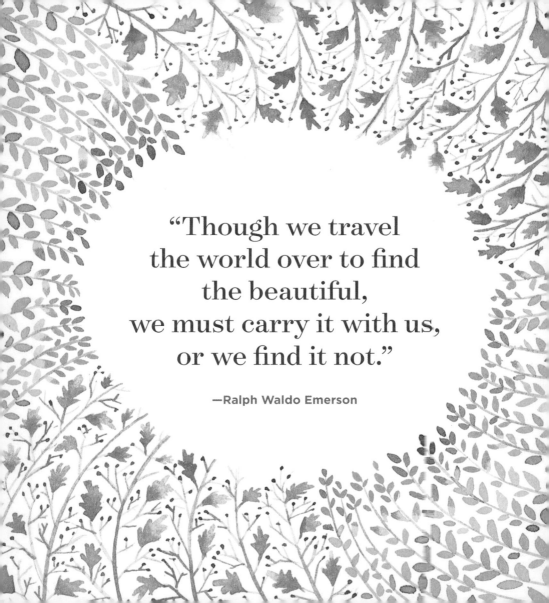

"Though we travel
the world over to find
the beautiful,
we must carry it with us,
or we find it not."

—Ralph Waldo Emerson

592. Read about British adventurer Austen Henry Layard's excavation of the ancient city of Nineveh (near modern-day Mosul, Iraq) in the 1840s.

593. Give second chances.

594. Learn how to build a roaring campfire (and the rules of creating and leaving one).

595. Make s'mores.

596. Toast grilled cheese on a stick.

597. Become an expert in something. It could be beekeeping, baseball statistics, Yosemite National Park, or anything that piques your interest.

598. Let life flow through you, and exist
in harmony with its ebbs and flows.
Ride the waves with equanimity,
knowing that you are the whole sea.

599. Walk in a place dominated
by traffic.

600. Go bobsledding.

601. Everybody has their own private Mount Everest that they were put on this Earth to climb. You may never reach the summit, but if you don't make at least one serious attempt to get above the snow line, you will regret it years later.

✿

602. As in the Japanese tradition, craft a *wabi-sabi* object, which is intentionally imperfect, impermanent, or incomplete.

✿

603. Let your hair be its natural color.

Wild List

Wild Things to Observe

Note how many different shapes of leaves
and textures of bark you see.

Look under rocks and fallen logs for insects,
fungi, and invertebrates.

Use a field guide to identify rocks and minerals.

Take pictures of birds you don't recognize.

Count the number of rabbits and squirrels.

Listen closely to birds and insects, the wind moving past
different leaves, and the sounds of earth underfoot.

Watch for butterflies.

Notice the different colors of soil.

Try to feel which way the wind is blowing.

604. Talk to plants.

❧

605. Sleep in the rain forest.

❧

606. Sweep away the junk at home,
at work, in your relationships,
and in your mind.

❧

607. Open a beer with a spoon.

608. Part your hair on the other side.

ও

609. Play paintball.

ও

610. Pack a backpack for roughing it, carrying only the essentials.

ও

611. Share a small tent in the wilderness with the one you love.

612. Think of overhauling your diet
as an adventure.

❧

613. Run away with the circus!
(Or just go to one!)

❧

614. Visualize walking through peaceful places.
Where do you end up? Can you incorporate
this visualization in your daily life?

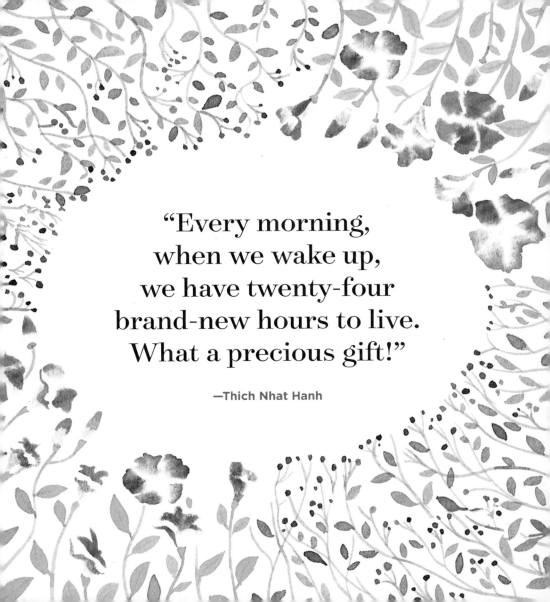

"Every morning,
when we wake up,
we have twenty-four
brand-new hours to live.
What a precious gift!"

—Thich Nhat Hanh

615. Take a leap of faith.

616. Milk a cow.

617. To live a more efficient life,
do things now, without procrastinating.
You will be amazed by how much better
you feel and by how much more
you accomplish.

618. A little fresh air and sunlight
can do wonders for the spirit. Treat yourself
to these whenever possible.

619. Take an after-dinner stroll.

620. Shop at an ethnic market.
Smell and taste whatever you can.

621. Learn how to walk a straight line
in the woods.

622. You can create allure by cultivating
mystery. Keep to yourself the name
of your perfume, the cost of your new car,
the location of your hideaway,
and your views on global warming.

623. Let people live vicariously through your adventures.

624. Splash in puddles.

625. Recruit a workout buddy.

626. Sketch what you see while riding on a train or bus.

627. Stay up past your bedtime.

628. Stand at the bottom of one
of the world's tallest skyscrapers
and look up.

629. List each year you have been alive,
and then in a word, sentence,
or short paragraph, write down
a significant memory from each year.

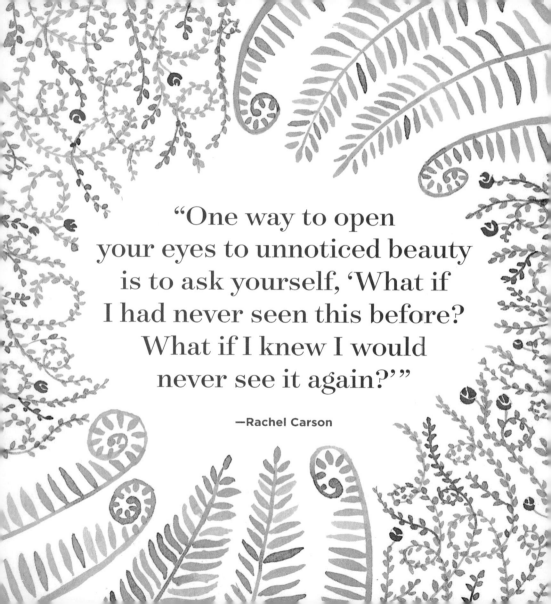

"One way to open your eyes to unnoticed beauty is to ask yourself, 'What if I had never seen this before? What if I knew I would never see it again?'"

—Rachel Carson

630. Learn to say "cheers"
in any language.

✿

631. Make eye contact with everyone
you meet.

✿

632. Walk closely with people you love
and with people who believe life
is a grand adventure.

✿

633. Trek the Himalayan foothills
in Myanmar.

634. Write a letter that matters
to you and that you know will make
a difference to the recipient.

635. Splurge on a facial.

636. Food tastes better when
you have grown it yourself.

637. Add a dash of joie de vivre
to every day.

638. Use only one hand to try
to button a shirt or get dressed.
Or use your feet to put something
in the laundry basket. This type of activity
rapidly expands circuits in the brain
that control tactile information.

ʎ

639. A journey must begin
with a single step.

ʎ

640. Use a woodburning kit to transform
a pumpkin into a jack-o'-lantern.

Destinations to Put on Your Bucket List

Alaska
Spruce shivering in empty loneliness, glassy glaciers,
looming mountains, salmon runs, treeless tundra

Antarctica
Frigid deserts, emperor penguins, a million shades
of blue, polar lights

Bhutan
Gross National Happiness, yak herders, temples and monasteries,
environmental protection, no tobacco

Greenland
Glaciers, reindeer, Viking ruins and runes, ice cores
and ice caps, fjords

Hawaii

Grass skirts, ukuleles, the hula, pineapples, volcanic fireworks, luaus, surfboards, outrigger canoes, fields of sugarcane

Hong Kong

Neon lights, markets, lantern festivals, skyscrapers, *A Symphony of Lights,* street food, Rolls-Royces

Iceland

Mountain huts, ponies, active geysers, volcanoes, waterfalls, glacier lagoons, friendliness, nature baths and thermal pools, colorful houses

Iguaçu Falls

275 towering waterfalls, rainbows above cataracts, monkeys, ocelots, 400 bird species, and coatimundi— like cuter, friendlier raccoons

Thailand

Silk, teak, coral reefs, long-tail boats, floating market vendors, fingernail dancing, Bangkok, friendliness, elephant polo

641. Celebrate your pet's birthday.

642. If you have nothing to lose,
you can try everything.

643. Revel in nature.

644. Go on a maple-sugaring tour.
Hang your own bucket to collect sap and
pick it up at the end of sugaring season.

645. Be a tourist in your own town. Get a fresh perspective on the place you think you know best.

646. Make your own trail mix.

647. Get paid for keeping your body strong by offering to rake leaves, walk dogs, mow lawns, shovel snow, or wash cars.

648. Enter a contest. You may win!

649. Dedicate a day to coloring books.

650. Make a crop circle.

651. Take a martial arts class.
It will challenge you physically
and mentally.

652. Tell someone how you really feel.

653. Cultivating a bonsai tree requires meticulous nurturing and training. Taking responsibility for its well-being makes you feel part of its peaceful world.

654. Pop a wheelie.

655. Culture yogurt at home.

656. Enjoy the satisfaction of mending a piece of clothing instead of throwing it away.

"In every walk with Nature
one receives far more
than he seeks."

—John Muir

657. Become a person who can solve problems in unexpected ways.

☙

658. Take a road trip making only left turns.

☙

659. Go to a farmers market with no list and invent a meal from whatever you find that looks, smells, and feels good.

☙

660. Expand your fitness horizons by joining an adult volleyball league or attending a yoga retreat.

661. A small seed can produce a large tree.

e

662. Practice looking with penetration at least five times today. Concentrate with all your being on whatever attracts your attention.

e

663. For a whole day, try to get by without saying yes or no.

e

664. Live and act from the understanding that all things change.

665. Make a list of the things you used to do that you no longer have the courage to do. Think about why you no longer do these things. If any are worth doing again, go for it!

e

666. Follow online extreme animal migrations, such as those of the bar-tailed godwit, monarch butterfly, krill, blue whale, Manx shearwater, lemming, bar-headed goose, arctic tern, wildebeest, or globe skimmer dragonfly.

e

667. Make a gourd birdhouse.

Wild List

Thing to Do if You Dare

Act confident. Faking it makes it real.

Be too busy to compare yourself with others.

Discard what you don't want to do. Change what you need to change.

Don't get married or have kids until you are sure you are ready.

Dream your dangerous dream.

Exercise your "risk muscle" at least once a day.

Pursue the career you love. The money you need will follow.

Dance on a table.

Stay away from people who belittle your passions.

Take quizzes and tests. Keep learning.

668. Make a special flip book
as a present.

669. Decorate a 365-page journal
as a new year's gift.

670. Try a new craft—glassblowing,
sculpting, woodworking, or whatever
appeals to you.

671. Accept your own definition
of what's right and wrong.

672. If you spend all your energy on reliving things that did not work, you will have no energy for finding new ways to be fulfilled. Let them go.

673. Notice patterns and make connections.

674. Decide that today is the first day of your new hobby. Look up how to get started on this potentially lifelong passion.

675. Go to an indoor ice-skating rink
in the summer.

676. Let a swing change the way you look
at your yard.

677. Go on a vision quest: Venture alone
into the wilderness for a few days,
and then fast and meditate.

678. Put together an envelope
filled with a letter, photos, magazine articles
or newspaper clippings, photocopies
of poems or passages from a novel, recipes,
and artwork. Stuff it so full that it is bursting
and mail it to someone special.

679. Rearrange your desk or the pictures
on your wall. These activities increase
your brain's alertness.

680. Skip class.

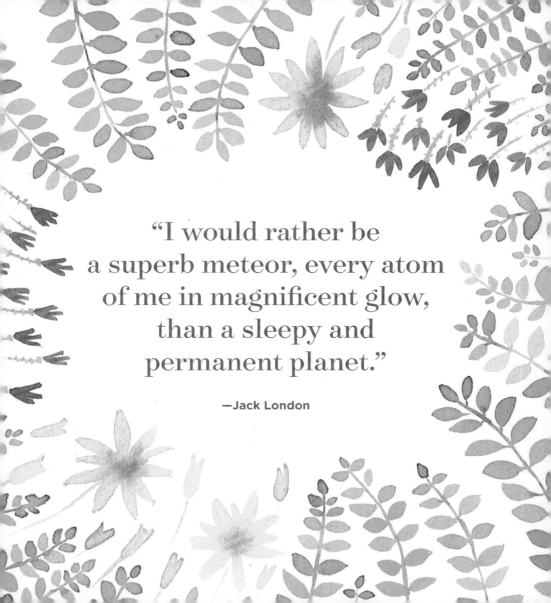

"I would rather be a superb meteor, every atom of me in magnificent glow, than a sleepy and permanent planet."

—Jack London

681. Water-ski.

682. Buy only what you need.

683. Visit all the major aquariums,
or focus on museums dedicated
to a particular area of interest,
such as art or science.

684. Do a cartwheel.

685. Ask people why they chose their jobs, what crossroads they have reached in their lives, and what their hopes and dreams are. You might learn something that is useful to your own path.

686. Become a squirrel or bird. Climb up a tree and sit there for an hour— or all day long.

687. Open up your eyes every day knowing it's another adventure, and it's all yours.

688. Look at the mark, not your arrow.

ᶾ

689. Be vigilant. Look at the stuff
you have surrounded yourself with
or the mental debris that has piled up.
Ask yourself: Does this make
me happy? Do I need this?
If you cannot answer yes,
then have the courage to let it go.

ᶾ

690. The next time you get some really
bad news, pop open a bottle of champagne.
This isn't about getting drunk.
It's about celebrating that endings
mean moving forward.

691. Perfect your golf swing.

692. Worship true eccentricity.

693. Roll down a sand dune
or hillside.

694. Appreciate the amazing
privilege it is to be alive,
to think, and to enjoy the world.

A Retreat to Create at Home

6–7:30 a.m. Spiritual practice (meditation, chanting)

7:30–8 a.m. Healthy breakfast

8–9:30 a.m. Exercise

9:30–10 a.m. Shower or bath

10–11 a.m. Creative writing or art session

11 a.m.–12 p.m. Study, reading, contemplation

12–12:30 p.m. Healthy lunch

12:30–2 p.m. Exercise

2–2:30 p.m. Spiritual practice

2:30–4:30 p.m. Cleaning
and cleaning out

4:30–5 p.m. Tea or coffee break

5–6 p.m. Spiritual practice

6–7 p.m. Creative writing
or art session

7–8 p.m. Healthy dinner

8–9 p.m. Study, reading,
contemplation

9–10 p.m. Spiritual practice

695. If you can create space and silence in your life to listen deeply, you may find you wish to help other people, bring love and compassion to them, and create positive transformation in the world.

696. Experiment with a cookie recipe—make a chewy version and a crispy one.

697. Sleep suspended above the forest floor.

698. Read an entire book about a country, culture, or religion that you know nothing about.

699. Share someone's pain today. Find a friend in distress and bear some of her grief.

700. Travel well instead of thinking about the importance of arriving.

701. Live life like a game.
Give yourself goals, but remember
that the true aim is to enjoy playing.

702. Wear sandals or flip-flops when
you shouldn't be wearing them.

703. Refuse to wear socks in winter.

704. Parade in Rio de Janeiro's Carnival.

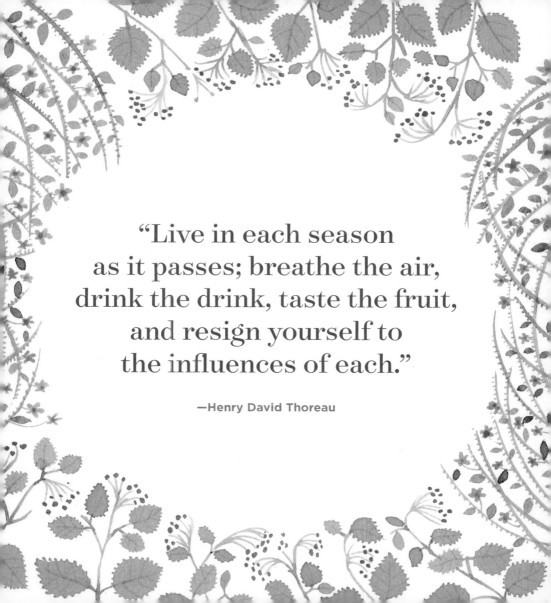

"Live in each season
as it passes; breathe the air,
drink the drink, taste the fruit,
and resign yourself to
the influences of each."

—Henry David Thoreau

705. Get lost in your favorite city.

706. Mail an anonymous gift card
to someone who needs it—an unemployed
friend, a college student, or someone
going through a major life change.

707. Read *The Adventures of
Huckleberry Finn* aloud to a ten-year-old.

708. "Pretend kidnap" someone on his or her birthday.

709. Ride a zip line.

710. Perfect a simple signature dish. Then make it for a dinner party.

711. You didn't fear crayons
in kindergarten.
Why fear them now?

ও

712. The past is gone and
the future is uncertain.
Today is your day.

ও

713. Rise at the crack of dawn to be
first in line for the ski lift.

714. Have your passport ready and, when you can, book a last-minute flight to another country.

ତ

715. Cook with an ingredient you've never used before.

ତ

716. Try to win prizes at a carnival.

ତ

717. Learn how to read a topographic map from the U.S. Geological Survey.

Children's Activities to Do as an Adult

Tell a Joke

Keep a list of your favorite jokes. Break them out
when someone needs a laugh.

Pet an Animal

Stop on the street to pet every dog and cat you see.
Get down on the floor for some quality playtime
with your house pet.

Arrange a Playdate

Get together with your kids, grandkids, nephews, nieces,
or other young relatives with the sole purpose of playing together.
Goofing around with kids helps you experience the joy
of play from their perspective.

Go Out

Arrange nights out with work colleagues. Go bowling
or miniature golfing, or play video games.

Play in the Sand
Go to the beach and bring your buckets and shovels.
Dig in as you did when you were five.

Hang Out With the Fun Kids
Surround yourself with playful people.
They'll help loosen you up and are more likely to support
and inspire your efforts to have fun.

Do Magic Tricks
Get a magic kit or take some lessons from a pro.
Put on a show in your living room.

Run Around Outside
Throw balls. Push kids on swings. Make mud pies.
Seesaw. See if you can still do the monkey bars.

Play Rainy-Day Games
Next time it's dreary outside, play cards or break out your old
board games. Do anything nonelectronic.

Sing
Listen to music and sing out loud. Play real instruments
if you have them; if not, go crazy on your air guitar.

718. Plant an herb garden.

719. Tie a helium balloon outside
your front door.

720. Approach new experiences as
opportunities to learn rather than occasions
to win or lose, succeed or fail.

721. Sell your stuff and hit the road.

722. Ask: What would nature do? Approach the natural world as a library of ideas rather than a warehouse of materials.

723. Play out a bad situation like a scene from a play. Choose your role and your dialogue and act out different scenarios to find the best way to move forward.

724. Stop the noise in your mind in order to hear the wonderful sounds of life.

725. Turn off the volume on the TV and you will come to view what you are seeing as somewhat ridiculous, neutral, or empty.

726. Learn to hula dance.

727. Micro-looking is the approach of the detective or the jeweler with a loupe. Use micro-looking to study a painting, an object, or nature.

728. Move to a totally new place.

729. Imagine that the way you walk
through life is the way you will be
walking through eternity. Think about
how you want to live forever
and start to live that way now.

730. Take a horseback ride on a beach.

731. Watch a laser show at a planetarium.

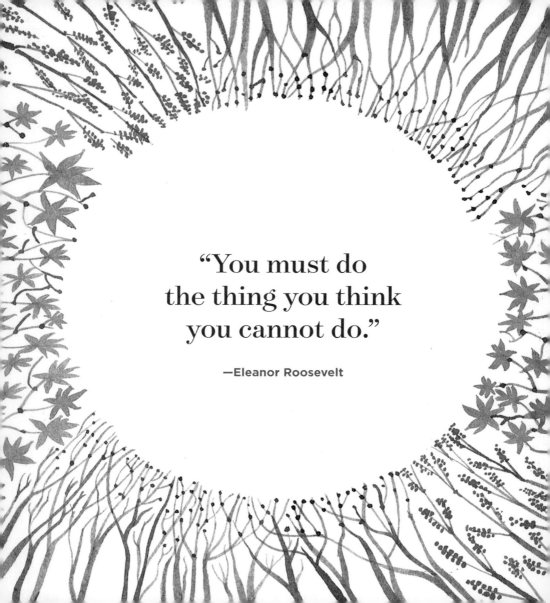

"You must do
the thing you think
you cannot do."

—Eleanor Roosevelt

732. Lift free weights for at least
five minutes every day.

❧

733. Respond to all messages
in 140 characters or less.

❧

734. Seek contemplative experiences
in the wild.

❧

735. Try high-adventure camping
on wilderness treks of a week or longer.

736. Keep some books with upbeat themes on your bookshelf to turn around negative feelings.

⟨

737. Throw open your mind's shutters and let the wind rush in. Brainstorm. Doodle. Think. Play. Daydream.

⟨

738. Using the mode of transportation that makes you happiest, go up a hill and then down really fast. The freedom of speeding downhill is quite exhilarating.

739. Make a small dream come true.

740. Slide down a sturdy banister.

741. Serenade someone. Even if you can't carry a tune, it's the thought that counts.

742. Build a backyard fort in the summer and an igloo in the winter.

743. Hop onto a train
(but never onto a moving car).

744. If you see a lost balloon
tied somewhere, set it free.

745. Have a barbecue in the middle
of a snowstorm.

746. Get a great fix-it manual
and learn to do basic home repairs.

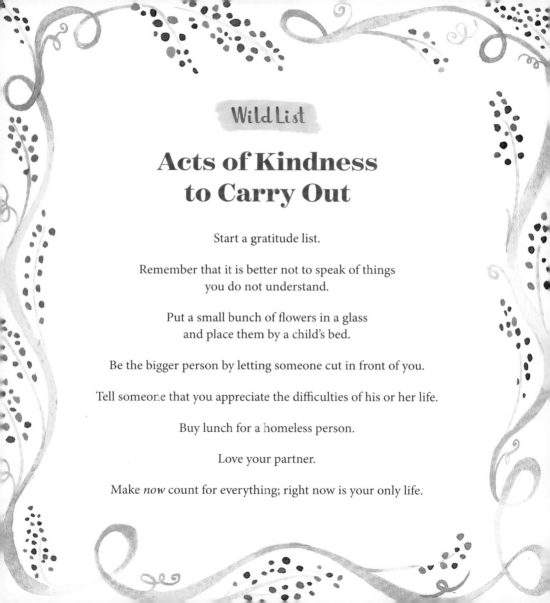

Wild List

Acts of Kindness
to Carry Out

Start a gratitude list.

Remember that it is better not to speak of things
you do not understand.

Put a small bunch of flowers in a glass
and place them by a child's bed.

Be the bigger person by letting someone cut in front of you.

Tell someone that you appreciate the difficulties of his or her life.

Buy lunch for a homeless person.

Love your partner.

Make *now* count for everything; right now is your only life.

747. Put on a play in your living room.

748. Preserve vegetation
for wild animals' food.

749. Fill your home with romance:
a fridge full of aphrodisiacs, mood music,
lighted candles, a bubble bath . . .

750. Kindness is an extraordinary
inner adventure.

751. Take a funny selfie with your head in a freezer or on top of a snowman.

752. In summer, jog or walk to the community pool, then swim for a period of time and walk or jog back home.

753. Go "indoor skydiving" in a vertical wind tunnel.

754. Go ice fishing.

755. Keep a running list of your
defining moments and review them
on a regular basis, even when you are not
faced with a major challenge or crisis.

756. Hijack someone's day and
take them out for a treat.

757. Learn how to do a flip turn
in a swimming pool.

758. Travel with no destination and simply focus on what you see, hear, and smell along the way.

759. Hike the Haute Route from Chamonix, France, to Zermatt, Switzerland.

760. Learn how to measure the distance you have walked using the "tally and pace" system, where 100 paces equals one tally. You can figure out how many tallies it takes you to walk a half mile. With experience, you can use time to measure the distance you have traveled.

"A ship in port is safe,
but that's not what ships
are built for."

—**John A. Shedd**

761. Bike solo on a beach path.

✿

762. Chaperone a child's field trip.

✿

763. Buy a lot of flower seed packets. Put the packets in random locations, hoping that whoever finds them will plant the seeds.

✿

764. Keep a notebook by your bed and record dreams as soon as you wake up. If you are curious, get a dream dictionary to help explain their meaning.

765. Learn how to make double
half hitch, square, and bowline knots.
You can use them to hold gear
on your pack, set up tents and
dining areas, and secure canoes and boats.
In emergencies, knots can hold bandages
in place and help in rescues.

e

766. Hug a tree and a person today.

e

767. Welcome spring by leaping into
traditional folk dancing.

768. Create something during the time you are doing your laundry and call it the "laundry project."

e

769. Rent a cottage or go "glamping" instead of spending your vacation at a resort or chain hotel.

e

770. Take a day trip on a steam train, enjoying this old-fashioned mode of travel.

e

771. Always find something to laugh at.

772. Go for a midnight paddle
under a full moon.

773. Make a Wikipedia page about
something you know everything about.

774. Take a 50-mile bike ride.
Train by starting with a mile and increasing
the distance until you reach the goal.

775. Listen to a music genre that
is outside your comfort zone.

Indoor Sports to Do Outdoors

Aerobics at a local park

Pickup basketball games

Bowling games: bocce, candlepin bowling, carpet bowls, pétanque

Dancing on the waterfront, in a park, or at a concert

Gymnastics on playground equipment or in a trampoline park

Pilates at the beach

Ping-Pong in the backyard

Volleyball on the beach

Weight lifting

Yoga on a dock by the water

776. Watch the movie *Bill & Ted's Excellent Adventure.*

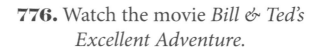

777. Observe an American bald eagle in the wild.

778. Learn how to throw an effective punch, escape from a choke hold, break out of a bear hug, and walk the streets safely.

779. On a cold, windy day, start your walk, run, or bike ride with the wind at your back. Then head into the wind for the second half of your workout. Your body will be warmed up and you will not feel as cold as if you had headed into the wind to start.

780. Go to the movies dressed like the characters in the film.

781. Connect with your partner in couples' yoga.

782. When you see a great recipe on a cooking show, buy the ingredients and cook it right away.

783. Skim a stone on one of the Great Lakes of North America.

784. Play a game at least once a month: Scrabble, bridge, poker, Battleship, Trivial Pursuit, Candyland, the Barbie Game, Monopoly, or Yahtzee, anyone?

785. Create a bucket list of animals to see in the wild (from a safe distance): grizzly bear, alligator, mountain lion, panda, peregrine falcon, toucan, puffin . . .

786. Walk the endless corridors of the Smithsonian museums in Washington, D.C.

"In the midst of winter,
I finally learned that
there was in me
an invincible summer."

—Albert Camus

787. Try to catch leaves as they fall from the trees in autumn.

788. Gallop across a field on horseback.

789. Launch a small rocket.

790. Read the book *Awake in the Wild,* by Mark Coleman, about mindfulness and nature retreats.

791. Pack a bugout bag in case of emergency.

⋑

792. Barter or swap services whenever possible.

⋑

793. Use chopsticks when you eat Asian food.

⋑

794. Learn to see desires and make smart choices rather than act on all of them.

795. Try to go a whole day without saying anything negative.

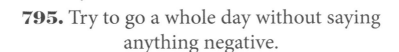

796. Meditation is the greatest adventure the human mind can undertake. It is to take delight in simply being—delight that comes from nowhere and everywhere.

797. A decadent way to usher in your next year of life: Throw an elaborate feast at the stroke of midnight on your birthday.

"Try to be a rainbow
in someone's cloud."

—Maya Angelou

798. Break into song and dance every now and then, just like in the old musicals.

ə

799. Lie on the ground on a clear night. Wait until you feel you have melted into the earth. Then convince yourself that the stars you are watching are below you. Gravity is keeping you on the earth, but the vast sky is down below.

ə

800. When you do what you love, it does not feel like work, and that is the most powerful motivator of all.

801. Race shopping carts.

802. What were your three favorites childhood activities? Do them.

803. Write an inspiring quote or joke on a dollar bill, hoping that someone will see it.

804. Destroy all the photos in which you think you look ugly.

805. Before you drive, start the car using only your sense of touch and spatial memory. Find the right key, buckle the seat belt, put the key in the ignition. You will find where these things exist in your brain.

806. Cycle the Kettle Valley Railway in Canada.

807. Order from a Vietnamese take-out menu by randomly picking five dishes and trying each thing that you order.

808. Study American Sign Language. It involves a wildly different way of communicating and it is beneficial to others.

809. Listen to a piece of music and try to identify the instruments playing.

810. There is nothing you cannot live down, rise above, and overcome.

Fears to Face

Clowns
Make friends with a clown or go to clown school.

Crowds
Go to a big-town parade, and if nothing bad happens . . .

Dark
Try to understand what in your childhood caused this fear.

Death
Pick a saying or quote that is meaningful to you, like:
"Death, therefore, the most awful of evils, is nothing to us,
seeing that, when we are, death is not come, and,
when death is come, we are not." (Epicurus)

Enclosed Spaces
Like the crowd scenario, try it, breathe deeply,
and see what happens.

Flying
Allow yourself to believe the facts: Statistically,
it's the safest mode of travel.

Heights
Gradually increase the height you can climb on a ladder.

Insects and Spiders
Knowledge is power. Learn to recognize the dangerous ones
and avoid them. Embrace the rest.

Public Speaking
What you said won't be remembered,
but your demeanor will be.

Snakes
Educate yourself to recognize them and know what to do
should you encounter one.

Swimming
Practice acclimating in shallow water. Take swimming lessons
and learn to hold your breath underwater.

811. Write your name in wet cement.

812. Never hold a meeting that lasts more than 30 minutes.

813. Seek a wilderness where even short walks offer stupendous views.

814. The more adventures one goes on in life, the more stories one has to tell.

815. Read *How to Be an Explorer of the World,* by Keri Smith.

816. Learn how to make pasta in Italy.

817. Learn about John James Audubon's travels up the Missouri River to sketch wild animals.

818. Visualize something wild, like a unicorn or Frankenstein's monster. Be as outlandish and original as you can. See what you can do with your mind.

819. Be an intellectual adventurer with a willingness to double back, ignore fences, or switch directions at the drop of a coconut.

❧

820. Carry the singing wilderness with you to the noisiest city.

❧

821. Climb a mountain or dive in an ocean to lose your sense of self and become one with nature. Immersed in the experience, your nonstop inner voice becomes quiet.

822. Take a scenic train ride to learn
more about the history of an area
and its landscape.

༈

823. Experiment in the kitchen.
Choose a cookbook to work through,
like in the movie and book *Julie and Julia*.
Choose a type of food you want to master.

༈

824. Buy something you have never
seen before at the grocery store.

"I have loved
the stars too truly
to be fearful
of the night."

—Sarah Williams,
"The Old Astronomer"

825. Explore the sky using
a stargazing app.

826. Compete in a 24-hour mountain
bike race under the midnight sun
in the Yukon.

827. Laugh to start your day.
Laugh when someone is mad at you.
Laugh when you drop something or
a machine misbehaves. Greet each
challenge with a smile or chuckle.
At the end of the day, let go
with some guffaws.

828. Make a nature diary and record the animals and plants you see while walking. You can take photos or make sketches of them and add notes when you get home.

❧

829. After staring at a computer screen all day, go outside and stare at the sky for the whole night.

❧

830. If you pick up but then put down a book at the bookstore, decide to buy it.

831. Eat with your eyes closed.
Have someone else prepare
the plate and then eat by smell,
taste, touch, and sound.

e

832. Host a "blind" wine tasting.

e

833. Become an amateur scientist
in an area that intrigues you,
from meteorology to astronomy.

Indulgences to Enjoy

A massage

Looking out the window

A walk through a botanical garden

A Sunday drive

An afternoon siesta

A hot bath

Lunch by yourself at a grand restaurant

An activity that is not constructive
or goal oriented

Daydreaming

An extra scoop of ice cream
in your cone

Revisiting your favorite piece
of music

Eating comfort food

Watching your favorite movie
for the 20th time

Drinking wine

Reading something that takes
your breath away

Smiling

834. Remember that many
of the major religions include
a crucial encounter with wilderness—
Moses, Jesus, and Muhammad
in the desert mountains,
Siddhartha in the jungle.

835. Learn how to read animal tracks
and scat to avoid crossing paths with
unfriendly creatures or to follow the trail
of something worth eating.

836. The best age-defying beauty
tip ever is: SMILE.

837. Seek out groups of like-minded people. Volunteer with political campaigns or other groups that focus on issues you care about.

838. Learn how to avoid being struck by lightning.

839. Find a path of footprints in the sand at the beach and walk the entire distance of the other person's walk.

840. Walk your dog on a new route.

🌿

841. Make your own fortune cookies
and write the fortunes inside.

🌿

842. Stop exploring only when
you've found heaven.

🌿

843. With a little creativity,
any environment can become your
fitness center: chin-ups on sturdy
tree branches, angled push-ups or
triceps dips on a park bench, walking lunges,
squats, side planks, crunches, and more.

"In the spring,
at the end of the day,
you should smell
like dirt."

—Margaret Atwood,
"Unearthing Suite"

844. Take up archery, a physical way of taking aim and eliminating distractions. Focus on the yellow, red, and blue circles and train your senses toward a single point.

ʅ

845. Change your perspective, which often is at eye level or lower. Look up and marvel.

ʅ

846. Use your best dishes at every meal.

ʅ

847. Challenge someone to an arm-wrestling contest.

848. Recognize and accept the healing
properties of chocolate.

849. Do tai chi in a park.

850. Run through a sprinkler.

851. Spend as much time outdoors
as you do indoors.

852. Lounge around a thermal pool under the midnight sun in Iceland.

853. Enter a 24-hour dance marathon for charity.

854. Build the ultimate blanket fort.

855. Make a funny short film and post it on YouTube.

856. Seek a throw-your-head-back-and-shout kind of freedom.

857. Snorkel or scuba dive to see a real shipwreck.

858. Prepare a breakfast from another country.

859. Skate backward.

Wild List

Challenges to Set for Yourself

Change.

End a bad habit.

Talk to a stranger.

Exercise for an hour every day.

Try a new recipe.

Study a topic you want to master.

Do something that scares you.

Meditate daily.

Conquer a daunting household task.

Throw away a misguided belief.

860. Enjoy two nights at a nice hotel in your area. It is a great extravagance minus the travel hassle.

ə

861. Be silly. Watch funny movies, comedy shows, comic strips, or anything that makes you laugh.

ə

862. Go sledding on a trashcan lid.

ə

863. Embrace being lost.

864. Donate blood.

865. Ride a unicycle.

866. Start a conga line.

867. Though travel is cool, living wild
is about experiences, not places.
An experience can cost nothing.
The ones you remember will have
changed you and brought
a smile to your face.

868. Walk barefoot on a pebbled path
if you have access to one,
and sense yourself grounded in
and connected to each moment.

869. Go for a boat ride.

870. Cook from scratch as often
as possible. You gain control over
the nutritional quality of your meals.

"May your trails be crooked,
winding, lonesome,
dangerous, leading to
the most amazing view."

—Edward Abbey

871. Overdress for the occasion.

◖

872. When you go to a foreign city,
just wander.

◖

873. Take yourself on a date.
Go out for a meal and to the event
of your choosing.

◖

874. People will judge you by
your actions, not your intentions.

875. Set goals to attain each week:
one sketch per day, one painting per week,
writing 1,000 words per day. Set these goals
to what you want, not what you think
you should do.

❧

876. Strap on a GoPro and tell the story
of a trip from your own viewpoint.

❧

877. Gather edible plants in the wild
each season, such as fruits and nuts.
Bring along a field guide!

878. Swap lunches with someone.

e

879. Spend a day working on a farm.

e

880. Learn to shear a sheep.

e

881. Put a mix of items in a container. Close your eyes and try to figure out what the items are using only your sense of touch. Because you normally use sight to distinguish between objects, your tactile abilities falter, like underused muscles.

"Today I have grown
taller from walking
with the trees."

—Karle Wilson Baker,
"Good Company"

882. Deliberately abandon a book with your name in it and see if anyone returns it to you.

❧

883. Do a good deed each day.

❧

884. Learn how to pack a perfect suitcase.

❧

885. Figure out your best jet lag remedy.

886. Vacation at a dude ranch.
Spend a week clearing your mind
and sharing an adventure
with four-footed companions.

887. Learn to tolerate silence.

888. Pick up a book that has been
sitting on your shelf for too long.
Read the whole thing.

889. Think less, do more.

890. Each time you exercise, step up the intensity. Exertion helps you let go. Enjoy the feeling of freedom.

891. Explore Rachel Carson National Wildlife Refuge in southern Maine.

892. Be a guerrilla gardener— plant vegetables on rooftops or on paved lots covered with compost, build small greenhouses, and grow things anywhere there is a patch of grass.

Fresh Ways to See the World

Snorkel
Explore a coral reef in the quiet of the underwater world.

Dogsled
Race through the snow-covered wilderness behind
a team of powerful canines.

Kayak or Canoe
Explore islands, bays, and coastlines at your own pace.

Llama Trek
Let this woolly pack animal lighten your load
on a walking expedition.

Bicycle
Peddle through the scenic countryside anywhere on Earth,
from Tuscany to Napa Valley.

Horseback Ride
Take a spectacular guided ride through Bryce
Canyon National Park.

Rock Climb
Quiet your mind with the concentration needed
for scaling rock walls and rappelling.

Thru-Hike
Hit the trails for a couple days in a rural area.

White-Water Raft
Led by an expert guide, feel the adrenaline as you rock
and roll through the rapids.

Ride a Camel
Experience nomadic life as you ride
through the desert.

Boat
Cruise a coastline and see nature
in a brand-new way.

893. Celebrate Chinese New Year.

894. Sit by the ocean just after sunset. Watch the horizon and note the exact moment when the horizon and ocean become indiscernible.

895. Ski on a glacier.

896. Learn about the Oscillation Overthruster in the movie *The Adventures of Buckaroo Banzai Across the 8th Dimension.*

897. Lighten up. You will live longer.

898. Cancel all your obligations
for the day for no other reason
than that you are happy.

899. Learn how to read palms.

900. Think about how you would like
to make your life more adventurous.
Then write down concrete steps
to make it happen.

901. Stare in awe at the stars.

ә

902. Be elated over a bird's nest in spring.

ә

903. Hunt for wild grapes or strawberries
in summer.

ә

904. Call an old friend, one you have
become completely distant from,
and try to start over.

905. Take time to smell the roses.

ɘ

906. Always buy lemonade from
a kid's lemonade stand.

ɘ

907. Remember that even famous artists,
writers, and musicians were not great
at everything—even within their own craft.

ɘ

908. Karaoke is an excellent way
to shed inhibitions.

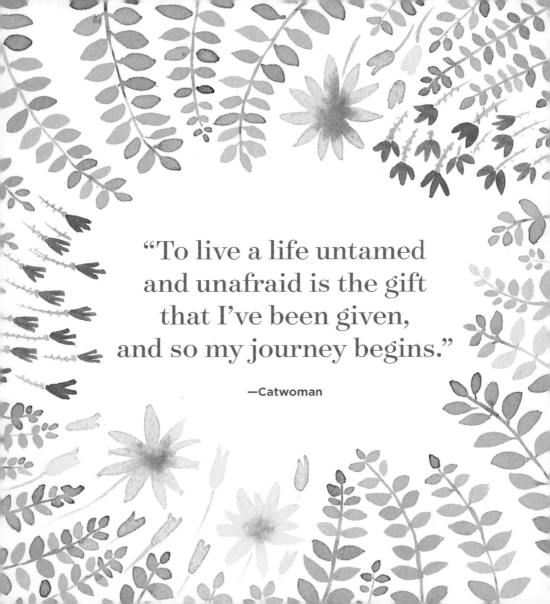

"To live a life untamed
and unafraid is the gift
that I've been given,
and so my journey begins."

—Catwoman

909. Eat like the French: Spread butter and jam on a baguette and drink café au lait from a bowl.

910. Engage in conversation with someone whose lifestyle and viewpoint differ from your own. Really listen to what they say.

911. Help someone today.

912. Practice until you have
a killer tennis serve.

◎

913. Make a flower arrangement
from flowers you picked yourself.
This act encourages you to look closely
at the miracle of the petals,
colors, and leaves.

◎

914. Put a funny sign on some item
of public infrastructure.
Stick around to see what happens.

915. Make a scrapbook with
a picture of every physical structure you
have lived in—from your childhood
home to your college dorms and beyond.

⊚

916. At meals, switch seats.
In most families, each person has his
or her "own seat." Changing positions
offers you a different perspective
on the room and even how
you eat your meal.

⊚

917. You cannot have an adventurous life
without taking chances.

Ways to Live Wild in Autumn

Gather fall leaves for a dried-flower arrangement.

View the foliage by bicycle instead of from a car.

Jump in leaf piles.

Take an outside photograph for your
family holiday card.

Pick pumpkins at a local orchard.

Find your way through a corn maze.

Count the geese flying in a V-formation.

Make a scarecrow.

Drink hot cocoa while walking outdoors.

Read a book in your favorite park.

Paint pictures of the brilliantly colored trees.

Collect pinecones to use in a wreath.

Walk country lanes to view the colors
and get lots of fresh air.

Set a series of hikes you want to accomplish
before winter.

Secretly plant tulip bulbs in a park.

Buy root vegetables at a farm stand
and make soup.

Run under a tree as the leaves fall.

Go on a hayride.

Watch a bonfire burn.

918. Pick one friend. Make a top-ten list of reasons why you think they are great. Send your friend the list through snail mail.

919. Appreciate those who cleared a path in the wilderness for civilizations to follow, who challenged accepted ideas about what is possible and what can be achieved.

920. Go skinny-dipping.

921. Play Ultimate Frisbee
or extreme croquet.

↖

922. Make a massive inspiration
board that fills a wall.

↖

923. Living wild does not mean
going on the most exotic, serious,
or expensive adventures. It can mean
seeking out and appreciating
all the little things.

924. If you want to make footprints in the sands of time, don't sit down.

925. Compose a poem and post it in a public place to brighten up someone's day.

926. For a week, trace the route of your excursions on a local map. Is your routine limited or wild and free?

"I believe great people
do things before
they are ready."

—Amy Poehler

927. Learn how to peel an orange
in one long peel. Pick a soft orange,
roll it around on a counter, and use your
thumb to puncture the peel near
the top or bottom of the orange.
Practice makes perfect!

࿇

928. Meet someone at the train station
with a picnic, a sweater, and sense
of adventure.

࿇

929. Sometimes you need to release your
mental burden and just say "forget it."

930. Watching wildlife can reawaken senses dulled by the man-made world.

ॐ

931. Pay attention to your circadian rhythm, your body's internal clock.

ॐ

932. Use a funny pseudonym when reserving a restaurant table or signing a guest book.

ॐ

933. Leap in the air and click your feet together to celebrate the pure joy of being alive.

934. The more you do your own thing, the less you confuse worldly rewards with spiritual rewards.

e

935. Experience the wind picking up, blowing the trees around wildly, then rain starting to pour, pounding you— without running for cover.

e

936. Learn how to prevent and survive a shark attack.

937. Eat fugu (puffer fish, blowfish, globefish) that has been prepared by an expert chef. The fish can be poisonous if the toxic innards are not properly removed.

e

938. Remain frugal. The less you can live on, the more chance you will succeed on your own terms.

e

939. Always be looking. Always be aware.

Ways to Live Wild
in Spring

Come out of hibernation and exercise outside every day you can.

Soak up the sun, even on still chilly days.

Take a mental health day off from work.

Brown-bag it outside on your lunch hour.

Have a picnic at the beach.

Drink coffee outside at a café.

Keep an eye out for the first crocuses, snowdrops, and daffodils.

Walk on a deserted beach before the crowds descend.

Go horseback riding at a local farm.

Set your alarm early to hear a full dawn chorus.

940. Opening the windows gives your mind raw material for creating new neural pathways.

941. Take a class in giving massages. This is a special gift you can share with your loved ones.

942. Read in bed until your arms hurt.

943. Ink a fake tattoo—
or get a real one!

944. Walk through a drive-through
instead of driving.

945. If you stay in the valley,
you will never go
over the hill.

946. Allow yourself to just be.

947. Remember that even
your work can be an adventure.
Explore ways to challenge yourself
and also add some play.

948. Step into the unknown
with all flags flying—
grow, adapt, and flourish.

949. For a day, avoid as many sources of electromagnetic energy as possible: high-voltage power lines, radio and TV towers, cell phone base stations, microwave ovens, and electric blankets. How do you feel?

950. Mountain and rock climbing may take everything out of you, but in exchange, you learn what you are made of.

951. Build a snowman in New York's Central Park.

"The race will go
to the curious,
the slightly mad, and
those with an unsated
passion for learning
and daredeviltry."

—Tom Peters

952. Get drenched in color
at India's Holi festival.

ʔ

953. Stand on your head.

ʔ

954. See how many different smells you
can identify on a nature hike.

ʔ

955. Compliment each person you meet on
one thing you genuinely like about them.

956. Linger in the tub.

957. The world is your cow, but you have to do the milking.

958. Take a nap in a field of wildflowers.

959. Taste a slice of pizza from every shop in town.

960. Travel from one end of a country
to the other.

961. Volunteer to be a magician's assistant.

962. Walk a pilgrimage to a place you
consider sacred, whether it's the birthplace
of a saint, the home of your favorite artist,
or a beautiful natural place.

963. Become a food rebel—refuse to eat processed and unhealthy food.

964. When you next spend time outside, enjoy the feeling of unlimited, airy space stretching in all directions.

965. If you usually wake up to the smell of freshly brewed coffee, put a scented candle or potpourri next to your bed. By waking to a new scent, you are activating new neural pathways.

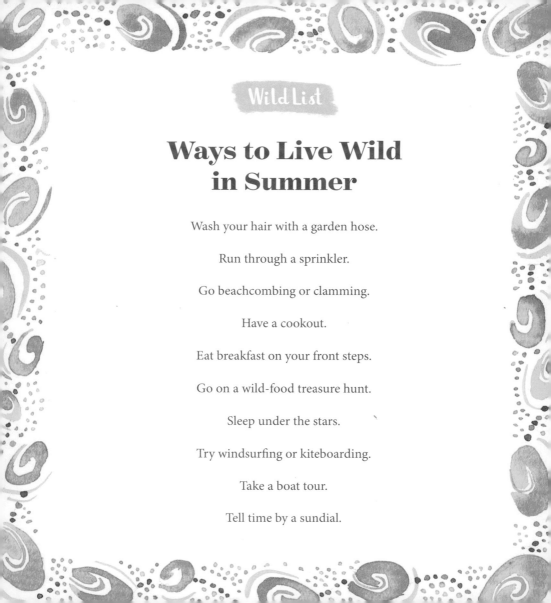

Ways to Live Wild in Summer

Wash your hair with a garden hose.

Run through a sprinkler.

Go beachcombing or clamming.

Have a cookout.

Eat breakfast on your front steps.

Go on a wild-food treasure hunt.

Sleep under the stars.

Try windsurfing or kiteboarding.

Take a boat tour.

Tell time by a sundial.

966. Learn how to play Frisbee golf.

967. Eat cereal for dinner and ice cream for breakfast.

968. In an airplane, close your eyes and imagine you are flying at hundreds of miles an hour and the airplane is not there.

969. Do a genetic test to learn
about your ancestry.

970. When you get stuck on a project,
get up and do something else.
The best ideas and solutions
emerge when you rest.

971. Dry shoes won't catch fish.

972. Be able to identify venomous
and poisonous insects.

973. Let a destination derail your schedule.
Go somewhere for a week and end up
staying for months.

974. Swim with sea turtles.

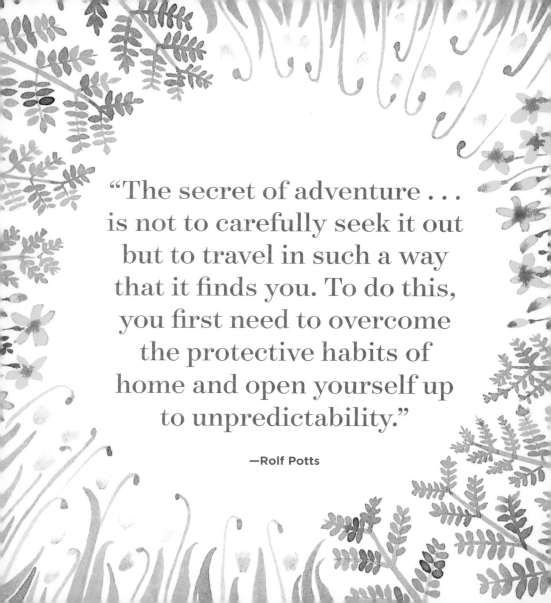

"The secret of adventure . . . is not to carefully seek it out but to travel in such a way that it finds you. To do this, you first need to overcome the protective habits of home and open yourself up to unpredictability."

—**Rolf Potts**

975. Feed a giraffe.

976. Swim under a waterfall.

977. Dive in a coral reef.

978. Ride a merry-go-round.

979. Smile at every single person you see.

e

980. Build a house with Habitat for Humanity.

e

981. Collect water from dewy grass, from bamboo, from a wet tree branch.

e

982. Build an upside-down snowman.

983. Watch an eclipse (safely).

❧

984. Take your greatest fear
by the ears and laugh in its face.
There is nothing more exhilarating.

❧

985. Set out to hear a lion roaring,
an elephant trumpeting, a glacier splitting,
wolves in the wild—all sounds heard
as beautiful music.

986. Sit down with a friend or significant other. Make a list of three new things you have "been meaning to do" together. Set the date for the first one.

987. Assess every project you propose by its wow factor.

988. Ask the wisest person you know to be your mentor.

Ways to Live Wild in Winter

Learn a new winter sport.

Build a snow fort.

Fly a kite on a particularly blustery day.

Have a snow picnic.

Visit a winter carnival.

Make snow angels.

Look for animal tracks in the snow.

Wrap up in a big coat and swing on a swing set.

Catch a snowflake with your tongue.

989. Have a Hopi sunrise naming for a baby or another ritual that celebrates the importance of nature in a baby's life from the very beginning.

990. Work from home one day a week.

991. Take a sabbatical.

992. Go to school with a kid.

993. Check out a job fair.

994. Take a photography workshop.

995. Try closing your nose
as you eat different foods. You will
experience information from the
texture and consistency alone.

996. Volunteer to be a Big Brother
or Sister for a needy child.

997. There is no need to kill time.
It dies by itself.

998. Design topiary in your yard.

999. Swim with whale sharks.

1,000. Train a Seeing Eye dog.

1,001. Look at every day as another adventure.

Acknowledgments

ɘ

Much appreciation to my editor, the fabulous Robin Terry Brown, and Tom Miller, my literary agent. They are wild enough to take a chance on me, and I am very grateful to both. I would also like to thank Francesca Springolo for her wildly imaginative illustrations. —BAK

About the Author

Barbara Ann Kipfer is a master listmaker and the author of more than 60 books, including the bestseller *14,000 Things to Be Happy About* (with more than a million copies in print), *The Order of Things, Self-Meditation, Instant Karma, 8,789 Words of Wisdom,* and *The Wish List.* She holds Ph.D.s in linguistics, archaeology, and Buddhist studies. Find out more about Kipfer at *thingstobehappyabout.com.*

READ. BREATHE. LAUGH.
with National Geographic Books

Experience all of life's pleasures with Daily Calm, Daily Joy, Daily Gratitude, and Daily Peace. In these elegant books, 365 days of stunning photographs are paired with meaningful reflections that will uplift and nurture you every day of the year.